Paws for Reflection

M.R. Wells
Kris Young
Connie fleishauer

HARVEST HOUSE PUBLISHERS

EUGENE, OREGON

Harvest House Publishers has made every effort to trace the ownership of all poems and quotes. In the event of a question arising from the use of a poem or quote, we regret any error made and will be pleased to make the necessary correction in future editions of this book.

Published in association with the literary agency of Mark Sweeney & Associates, Bonita Springs, FL 34135.

The information shared by the authors is from their personal experience and should not be con-sidered professional advice. Readers should consult their own dog care professionals regarding issues related to the health, safety, grooming, and training of their pets.

Cover photo © George Doyle / Stockbyte Photography / Getty Images

Cover by Left Coast Design, Portland, Oregon

PAWS FOR REFLECTION
Copyright © 2009 by M.R. Wells, Kris Young, Connie Fleishauer
Published by Harvest House Publishers
Eugene, Oregon 97402
www.harvesthousepublishers.com

Library of Congress Cataloging-in-Publication Data
    Wells, M.R. (Marion R.).
    Paws for reflection : devotions for dog lovers / M.R. Wells, Kris Young, Connie Fleishauer.
       p. cm.
    ISBN 978-0-7369-2574-7 (pbk.)
    1. Dog owners—Prayers and devotions. I. Young, Kris. II. Fleishauer, Connie. III. Title.
    BV4596.A54W455 2009
    242—dc22

                            2009000599

*To our heavenly Father,
our earthly parents,
and all those whose stories we
were allowed to share.*

Without you, this book wouldn't have happened.

Paws for Thanks

Dogs are pack animals, and for this book, we coauthors have been too. We have dipped from a wide pool of stories generously shared by family and friends. We are so grateful to all the humans and canines whose experiences have enriched these pages.

Special thanks to our agents, Mark and Janet Sweeney, for sharing our vision and helping it to happen; to Nicole Overbey, DVM, and Jonathan Klein, for their feedback and suggestions; and to our marvelous team at Harvest House Publishers, especially our wonderful editor, Barb Gordon.

Most of all we thank and praise God, who in His inscrutable wisdom gave us dogs to love—and to love us back.

Contents

Part 1
Paws for Love
Curl Up with the Master

Part 2
Paws for Training
Sit, Stay, Grow

Part 3
Paws for Healing
Let God Smooth Out the Tangles

Part 2
Paws for Guidance
Follow Your Alpha

Spiritual Snapshots

God has always spoken to us in visuals. The Bible is filled with them. Faith is Noah building an ark. Obedience is Abraham laying his son Isaac on an altar. Deliverance is Daniel standing unharmed in a den of hungry lions. In these and myriad other images, in the festivals God gave His people, in the lives of His prophets and even their dreams, God paints scenes that serve as "spiritual snapshots" of His truths. And in the ultimate spiritual snapshot, Jesus died on the cross to show us both the wages of sin and the unspeakable love and mercy of God.

Though the Bible was completed many centuries ago, God still speaks to us in "spiritual snapshots" today. They are everywhere in His creation and in our lives. We believe some of these snapshots are dog-shaped, and we have created an album of them for you. What does God's redemption look like? Maybe like a "bad hair day" homeless dog being scooped off a country road into a warm, loving family. What does clinging to God's promises look like? Maybe like a pup stuck in the ice, eyeing and smelling her master's wool cap that he left to comfort her and reassure her he'd return. What does a miracle of restoration look like? Maybe like a phone call that a dog lost for months and despaired of never being returned has been found—in answer to prayer.

If the dogs in our stories spoke English, they'd join us in inviting you to browse their album. They'd hope their stories inspire you to see spiritual snapshots in your own life and in your pets' lives. And they would pray that just as they've soaked up their masters' love and care, you will bask in the love of your Master—now and forever.

The Authors and Their Pups

M.R. Wells

A reddish-tan and cream Pomeranian fox, **Becca** is so full of life I call her my "Energizer Bunny dog."

Biscuit mixes cover-dog looks with a Miss Congeniality temperament.

Part sheltie, part "potluck," and all personality, **Morgan** is a shy guy with a heart of gold.

Kris Young

Sweet-natured and a little goofy, **Gracie** had an uncanny ability to read my mind.

Connie Fleishauer

Full of energy and affection, **Jack** loved going out in the fields and swimming in irrigation ditches.

Mandy weighed only one pound when she came to us, but she quickly won our hearts.

Small in stature but large in faithfulness, **Max** often behaved like a tiny, proud lion.

A "bad hair day" dog with a crazy, goofy attitude, **Squitchey** is always quick to make us smile.

Stuart is strong and active. He loves being with us—wiggling, cuddling, and licking our ears.

Part I

Paws for Love

Curl Up with the Master

 ROSIE

The Worth of a Dog
Redemption Is Priceless

*Your worth consists in what you are
and not in what you have.*

THOMAS A. EDISON

Big Frank's heart went out to the little one-year-old Sheltie mix "owned" by some rough friends of his. Four months went by before they even bothered to name her. This was only one of a number of clues Frank had that this wonderful pooch was of little value to these guys. It bothered him even more when he learned they'd decided to call the dog "Squirt" because when their rowdy pals came over, she got so nervous she "leaked." Frank kept his eye on Squirt and told himself if he ever got the chance, he'd rescue the dog and give her a new name.

That opportunity presented itself a couple of months later when Squirt got really sick. No one wanted to spend money to help her get well. Big Frank made his move. He'd take the dog to the vet, and he'd pay the bill—with the stipulation that the dog would then be his. Squirt's masters readily agreed.

Frank took his new dog to the vet and asked him to do whatever it took to fix her up. Soon his new pup, "Rosie," was in glow-ing good health. Sensing Frank's love for her, Rosie blossomed in confidence and self-esteem and became his loyal canine com-panion for many years, secure in the love of a master who valued her greatly.

In my life, one of the things I valued highly as a kid was comic books. Forget candy and saving for college—I was spending all my hard-earned nickels and dimes on the coolest literature in the world. D.C. and Marvel comic books had the power to transport me to other dimensions where I could vicariously fly, see through walls, and battle aliens with budding superpowers. I recall walking to a local "mom and pop" store and buying my fresh-off-the-press copy of Fantastic Four #1. Even then I was meticulous about keeping my treasures neat and clean. I'd post hand-drawn warn-ing signs on my "strong boxes," promising doom to anyone who dared touch my cache—such as my rough-handed, snotty-fingered little brother and sister. I planned on stockpiling the comic books, hoping I'd be a King Midas Jr., and they'd turn to gold.

One day I came home to find my priceless collection gone! I was in a panic. What manner of thief steals a little boy's comic books? I ran to my mom, and before I could tell her of the grue-some crime she confessed to dumping the whole lot because I hadn't cleaned my room. She told me not to bother digging in the trash. The garbage truck had taken them away while I was at school. As my jaw hit the floor like a dropped bowling ball, the villainess said maybe next time when she told me to clean up, I'd listen. I was aghast. She was equating my most valuable posses-sions on earth with…garbage. Clearly what she valued was very different than what I did.

During the decades that have gone by since, I've occasionally reminded her of her injustice. I've pointed out that now a nice copy of Fantastic Four #1 might fetch enough to buy a new BMW. But she still answers the same way and without a trace of remorse: "You should've cleaned your room."

Back in the day, I was willing to plunk down 100 percent of my weekly allowance for comic books that, to my mom, were as worthless as yesterday's newspapers. Many years later, Big Frank was willing to pay whatever it cost to redeem a dog another household readily sold for the price of a vet bill. As these two very different situations illustrate, clearly value is at least partly in the eye of the beholder.

And so it is with human beings. We often differ in how we behold the value of one another. While our parents may always see us as their precious little babies, others may view us as dull, forgettable, and worthless. Even worse, we may agree with them and wonder, like George Bailey in the classic film *It's a Wonderful Life*, why we were even born. When we begin to believe low-ball assessments of our worth, it's essential to check out what our Owner's Manual—the Bible—says about our value. Psalm 139:13-14 reminds us, "For you [God] created my inmost being; you knit me together in my mother's womb. I praise you because I am fearfully and wonderfully made; your works are wonderful, I know that full well."

That's the truth straight from our Creator's mouth. He says we're not only wonderful, but "wonderfully made." Still, in a world that doesn't affirm this, I often forget the truth and start believing that my value is determined by my works, by the things I do. When my writing is rejected or highly critiqued, the fragile biplane that is my self-esteem nosedives into a tailspin. The only solution to a never-ending loop of crash landings in the valley of despair is to shut my ears to the voices of the world, where my worth is determined by what people say about me and my latest success, and open my ears to who God says I am and what I'm worth. If value is determined by what someone is willing to pay, then God, who paid for us with the life of His Son, Jesus, believes we are priceless. And He dearly loves us forever!

For you know that God paid a ransom to save you from the empty life you inherited from your ancestors. And the ransom he paid was not mere gold or silver. It was the precious blood of Christ, the sinless, spotless Lamb of God (1 Peter 1:18-19 NLT).

Consider This

What do you treasure most in your life? If it were taken from you, how much would you be willing to pay to redeem it? Do you value yourself as much as God values you? If not, why not?

A Child of the King
God's Love Transforms

*God loves each of us as if
there were only one of us.*

St. Augustine

Our house is on a nice, calm, country road. I drive on it at least once a day. It's lined with big trees and comfortable homes. I can see sheep, goats, horses, and cows in the fields. Once in a while I have to slow down while a peacock crosses the road. But until one specific week, I'd never noticed the small, determined, "bad hair day" puppy. She chased my car for a few days in a row. She would run into the middle of the road in front of my car and bark. I'd stop, look at her, wait for her to get out of the way, and then drive on. But one day, out of concern for her safety, I stopped, got out, and called her. She came reluctantly. I picked her up and saw how dirty and unkempt this little gal was. I took her to the nearest house where I assumed she lived. The man who opened the door said she wasn't his, although she'd been sleeping in his backyard and eating the dog food out there. He'd listed her in the paper and put posters up, but no one claimed her. He told me if I wanted her, I could have her. I thought I might, but I needed to ask my husband, Steve, first.

To my amazement, when Steve heard my story he said he'd always thought he'd like to have a dog like that. In all our 35 years of marriage, I never dreamed that a wiry little long-haired terrier-type pup would be on his want list.

The next day I took my granddaughter Sierra along to pick up this funny-looking new addition to our family. The kind man wasn't sure she could learn our ways. He thought she was an out-door dog and wouldn't like being inside. He also thought she'd wander back to his house. He said if that happened, he'd call us. We thanked him and carried her away.

Our first task was to name our new dog. Sierra suggested Evie. We tried calling her that, but it didn't seem to fit. A few days later my daughter Karen came to spend the weekend. She held our dog, looked her over, and said, "When I studied at Oxford in England there was a street I often saw. I promised myself that some day I'd have an animal that fit the street's name. This is the critter! The street's name is Squitchey."

Looking at this "bad hair day" dog that was full of spirit and energy, we knew Karen was right. Our dog now had her name. The next concern was how she was adjusting to us and our home.

She was doing just fine, thank you very much. Squitchey thrived in our loving family. It took her no time at all to make friends with our Welsh corgi, Stuart. She loved being in the house and found her own private sleeping place, though she also adored sitting on any of our laps. She had a bit of a problem letting us know when she had to go out to "do her business," but for Christmas we got her a doggie door. She took to it right away. She ran outside, barked at the birds, did her thing, and came back in.

Squitchey has never wandered away as the man feared she

would. She's accepted her new life and enjoys living as a doggie princess with her doting new masters. Her life was transformed by love.

So was Natalia's.

She was an orphan in Russia. My niece Cindy and her husband, Jerret, had felt for some time God was leading them to adopt a child. They already had three wonderful sons and a beautiful daughter, so they could offer a big, loving family to a child who had none. The entire family would love her, care for her, and tell her about Jesus.

To get Squitchey, all I had to do was drive down my neighborhood road, make sure she didn't have a master, and bring her home. Cindy and Jerret had to go through far more. It took four trips to Russia and a lot of hard work and sacrifice. But they were obedient to God's call, and He blessed them with a lovely girl.

Natalia went from a crowded orphanage to a warm, wonderful home filled with love for her and for God. Some of her first English words were from songs sung in church and Sunday school. She became part of the family, the church, and the community. Once she understood more English, she learned how Jesus loved her, died for her, and rose again to prepare a home for her in eternity. She responded to His love and prayed, giving her life to God through faith in Jesus Christ.

It took Natalia a while to trust her new family, but their love transformed her. She accepted her new role as their much-loved princess. And she also learned to trust God's love and is now an official daughter of the King!

Squitchey knows she belongs to us, and we won't let anyone hurt her. She knows she's safe in our love. I believe that's why she doesn't run off. Natalia feels protected in her new home, and she knows her family loves her and will never leave her. She also knows she will be in heaven for eternity, living with her heavenly Father and King.

Unlike a human family, God's family has no limits. He is waiting to embrace all people who are wandering homeless. He is waiting to embrace all those who are spiritual orphans. He welcomes all who give their lives to Him through faith in Christ. We are His beloved children, and He will shower us forever with His transforming love.

In love he predestined us to be adopted as his sons through Jesus Christ, in accordance with his pleasure and will (Ephesians 1:4-5).

Consider This

Are you a child of the King? If so, how did you come to join His family? What are some important ways His love has transformed you? Have you shared His love with others? How have they responded?

If you haven't yet joined God's family, what is stopping you? Why not talk to God right now about it?

The Right "Spin" on Worship
Be Yourself with God

Almost all absurdity of conduct arises from
the imitation of those whom we cannot resemble.

SAMUEL JOHNSON

My friend Michael recently crossed the finish line of an excruciating divorce. One of the most painful aspects was deciding custody rights for their children. But one thing the courts didn't weigh in on was the custody of Mango, the family's beloved boxer. Mango had been Michael's gift to his wife, so the dog went to live with her. Now Michael only sees Mango when he picks up his kids.

If "absence makes the heart grow fonder" is true for humans, it's even truer for dogs. Mango goes nuts the minute she sees Michael. She spins in delirious circles, races back and forth across the yard, and ends by spinning again. Mango's nutty celebration of Michael's return always warms his heart. It lets him know she still loves him. Mango's "happy dance" is always the same: spin, run, spin. Michael told me wild and crazy spinning is characteristic of the boxer breed. It's how they're wired to express joy.

My wife, Celine, is wired to express joy in a "Mangoesque"

way. She comes from the demonstrative Filipino culture, and her family embodies that. When Celine got the phone call that told her she'd landed her dream job—teaching at a school minutes from our house—she screamed loudly enough to be heard in the Philippines! Then she jumped up and down like a cheerleader, grabbing and hugging everyone in sight.

In contrast, I'm a quiet and inscrutable Chinese-American guy. I have roots in an ancient culture known for being emotionally reserved. I'm wired to express joy quite differently than Mango and Celine. I don't spin. I don't jump. I don't race across my yard. I don't do cartwheels or pump my fist in the air and scream "Yes!" For the most part, I express my joy internally. All you might see on the outside is the hint of a smile. But on the inside—hey, look out! I sometimes spin like a complete idiot and do wind sprints back and forth across the backyard of my brain.

That's why when it came to worshiping God and expressing joy in Him, I used to feel self-conscious around more demonstrative believers. There were certain churches and events where I felt out of place. All these people were deliriously clapping, raising their hands in the air, swaying to the beat, some even doing human versions of the boxer spin. And then there was me...quietly doing my internal worship thing. I occasionally clapped but, being rhythmically challenged, I would soon lose the beat. Feeling great pressure to conform, I'd halfheartedly raise my hands, but I felt like an impostor.

I was really sunk when they'd do children's worship songs that were accompanied by "fun" movements, like a spiritual version of "I'm a Little Teapot." As I looked around at all the smiling, happy faces of uninhibited adults, I wondered if there was something wrong with me. Could it be that, like the Tin Man in *The Wizard of Oz,* I didn't have a heart?

No, that wasn't the case at all. As I steadfastly read my Bible, prayed, walked in the mountains memorizing Scripture, and spent time with my Creator in silent meditation, I realized that this was worship too. I'm wired to express joy differently. I'm not a boxer Christian, and that is okay. God doesn't look at externals. He looks at our hearts when we worship. Just as ice cream lovers enjoy different flavors, I believe God takes pleasure in the different varieties of worship offered by His children.

I was encouraged when I noticed the Bible describes different types of worship. King David seemed to engage in boxer-type worship. In 2 Samuel 6:14 it says, "David, wearing a linen ephod, danced before the LORD with all his might." I think in twenty-first-century terms, David was dancing in the streets in his boxers. David's wife Michal didn't approve of that. Second Samuel 6:16 says, "As the ark of the LORD was entering the City of David, Michal daughter of Saul watched from a window. And when she saw King David leaping and dancing before the LORD, she despised him in her heart."

Michal also criticized David to his face. He defended himself by saying he was celebrating "before the LORD." Apparently God sided with David because right after his comments the Bible notes that Michal was childless till the day of her death.

Scripture also shows us worship at the other end of the spectrum—a flavor as different as vanilla is from chocolate. In Luke 2:17-19 NLT we read, "After seeing [the baby Jesus], the shepherds told everyone what had happened and what the angel had said to them about this child. All who heard the shepherds' story were astonished, but Mary kept all these things in her heart and thought about them often."

Mary's joy was inward. She thought about and meditated on the miracle that had taken place. If anything was worth spinning over or clapping and raising one's hands about, it would be giving birth to the Savior of the world. It would be realizing you are the woman chosen to bear the Messiah. And yet Mary simply "kept all these things in her heart."

Each of us is wired to express our joy and love for God differently. The Lord takes delight in our various flavors of worship. Whether we spin or sing or lift hands or quietly rejoice in our hearts, if we worship Him in spirit and in truth, God will be well pleased with us.

Yet a time is coming and has now come when the true worshipers will worship the Father in spirit and truth, for they are the kind of worshipers the Father seeks. God is spirit, and his worshipers must worship in spirit and in truth (John 4:23-24).

Consider This

How do you express joy in daily life? How do you worship God? Do you feel pressure to worship like those around you? How can you encourage others to be themselves and worship in spirit and truth?

Left Behind
Keep Trusting God

Every tomorrow has two handles.
We can take hold of it with the handle of
anxiety or the handle of faith.

HENRY WARD BEECHER

There is a wonderful bond of trust and love between Pastor Sam Adams and his black-and-white border collie named Laska. On one particular day, it would be tested in a way Sam never expected.

Sam, his wife, their three small children, and Laska were going from their home in Bend, Oregon, to a church retreat on the Oregon coast. As they were heading over Santiam Pass, Sam pulled the vehicle over so his wife could change their baby's diaper. While they were waiting, Sam and Laska got out of the car. Sam threw a pine cone for his dog to retrieve. At some point Sam was distracted and lost track of his dog. And Laska probably ambled off to gnaw on his pine cone. Sam still isn't quite sure how it happened, but the family jumped back into the car and took off, leaving Laska behind. Not until half an hour later did Sam realize, in a moment of panic, that their dog wasn't with them.

Sam's wife was driving then. She turned around and drove back so fast one of their young sons lost his lunch. When they reached their previous stopping place, Laska was nowhere in sight. Then they spotted a note posted on a roadside sign. It said a dog had been found and included a phone number. Sam and his family were soon reunited with Laska, whose rescuer told them their dog had been sitting patiently by that road sign, waiting for his masters to come back.

Because he is human, Sam knows he's not perfect. He can have momentary memory lapses when a treasured pet or human can briefly drop off his radar. Not so with God! He *never* loses track of His own. Still, things happen that may make us feel "left behind" by our heavenly Master. And when they do, God calls us to sit and wait patiently for Him.

Sam experienced such a "left behind" time just after he'd finished getting his master's degree at Fuller Seminary. He had a house and church position lined up. He was looking toward getting a Ph.D. as the next step in fulfilling his dream of ministering for the Lord. Then family needs came up that had to be taken care of. This meant returning to the eastern Sierra and taking a job in construction.

Sam felt as though all his dreams were pulled out from under him. He had no official ministry and saw no opportunity for one. But he did have a loving, trusting relationship with the Lord. As Laska would do years later, Sam felt called to sit and wait.

Laska waited for only an hour. Sam waited for months. Finally the church his family attended asked Sam to lead communion on a Sunday. He would have just ten minutes to minister and share, but he eagerly accepted this opportunity. The night before he was to speak, he got another call. The person slated to preach the next morning had cancelled. Could Sam take over?

Sam could and did! The church people enjoyed his message. They had recently lost their teaching pastor, and Sam wondered if he might be tapped for that position. Hope flickered. But the post was never offered. Once again Sam was faced with sitting and waiting for his Master. Once again he obeyed.

God began to impress on Sam that when dreams are dashed, He will bring life. He's a God of resurrection. Learning this lesson "by the roadside" gave Sam the strength to continue waiting for God's leading.

Time passed. One day Sam received a surprise phone call from a relative. Had he considered moving to Bend, Oregon? Had he thought about ministering there? Sam's relative offered $400 of expense money to drive up and check the situation out. For a brief moment it seemed this new hope would be dashed too. Sam discovered two of his car tires were too bad to make the trip, and he couldn't afford to buy new ones. But his relative sent $300 more than promised without knowing Sam's need. Making the trip, Sam checked everything out and then moved his family to Bend. He planted the River Mennonite Church, which he still pastors.

Recently God also opened the door for Sam to augment his training by taking correspondence courses with a well-known seminary in Scotland.

Sam points out that 2000 years ago, when Jesus died on the cross, His closest followers probably felt left behind too. How could Jesus' kingdom come now that He'd been crucified? How could the world change? What would they do without the One they had followed for three years?

One of the things they did, despite other stumbles, was to keep the Sabbath. In Luke 23:55-56 we read, "The women who had come with Jesus from Galilee followed Joseph and saw the tomb and how his body was laid in it. Then they went home and prepared spices and perfumes. But they rested on the Sabbath in obedience to the commandment." Jesus' close disciples must have done the same. They sat and waited and obeyed God the best they knew how.

After that horribly painful Sabbath, they returned to the tomb on Sunday and discovered, to their wonder and delight, that Jesus had risen!

If we resist the temptation to wander and wait obediently for God, He will prove His faithfulness in our lives.

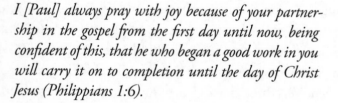

I [Paul] always pray with joy because of your partnership in the gospel from the first day until now, being confident of this, that he who began a good work in you will carry it on to completion until the day of Christ Jesus (Philippians 1:6).

Consider This

Can you remember a time when you felt left behind by God? What were the circumstances? How did you respond? What happened? How can you use what you learned to encourage someone who is feeling lost?

Back from the Dead
Hope in God's Restoration

*If you do not hope, you will not find
what is beyond your hopes.*

St. Clement of Alexandria

We were expecting Tim and Lisa to be arriving for our weekend retreat, so their phone call that Saturday morning stunned us. They weren't coming, and they desperately needed our prayers. Elsa, their beloved Rottweiler puppy, was missing from their yard. It was possible the gate was left open, but they thought it more likely she'd been taken. Though some Rottweilers are trained as guard dogs, Elsa was too young and hadn't had any such schooling. She was sweet and gentle, and someone could have easily grabbed her. Tim and Lisa were heartsick at the loss of their little girl. As they scoured their neighborhood, we begged God to have the pup restored to them.

We continued to plead for Elsa over the next days and weeks, but Tim and Lisa found no trace of her. She'd been microchipped so her owners could be found even if the tags had somehow been lost off her collar. But no one contacted them or responded to their inquiries or lost dog flyers. Gradually hope faded. Maybe Elsa wasn't physically dead, but she was dead to them. They grieved deeply and clung to Psalm 34:17-18: "The righteous cry out, and the LORD hears them; he delivers them from all their troubles. The LORD is close to the brokenhearted and saves those who are crushed in spirit." Eventually Tim and Lisa located a rescue group who had a female Rottweiler puppy in need of a home and welcomed this new dog into their family.

Six months after Elsa had gone missing, Tim and Lisa's phone rang. Someone had their dog! Although Tim and Lisa lived in a westside suburb of Los Angeles, Elsa had been found wandering downtown…miles away. She was still wearing her original collar and tags, and they had led her rescuer to Tim and Lisa. Overjoyed, they welcomed Elsa "back from the dead" and gratefully praised God for this miracle of restoration in their lives.

Restoration can take many forms. I saw God do a miracle of a different type when He brought my mom "back from the dead." She'd battled chronic leukemia for years and had been hospitalized for pneumonia. Soon after she came home, I spoke with her on a Sunday afternoon. Everything seemed to be all right, so I was totally unprepared when a frantic call came from one of her caregivers. Mom's lungs had filled with fluid, and she was being rushed to the hospital. The caregiver advised me to drop everything and get to the hospital as soon as possible.

Mom lived in Santa Barbara, 90 miles from my Los Angeles home. I was still half an hour away when my cell phone rang. Mom was in the emergency room, the medics were working on her, and the situation was serious. I might have some tough decisions to make.

"Can you keep her alive till I get there?" I begged. The doctor wasn't sure.

I'd managed to make some quick calls to activate some prayer chains—people willing to pray and call someone else, who would also pray and call the next person on the list. I'd been praying in the car and continued to do so as I covered those last miles. Mom was still breathing when I reached her. She seemed somewhat aware of my presence. Incredibly she was doing a tiny bit better.

The suspicion, which was later confirmed, was that Mom had suffered a severe heart attack. A cardiologist had been assigned to her case. He recommended more tests. They showed she probably had blockages, but because of her age and condition, surgery was considered too high-risk for the moment. Mom was put in ICU on a ventilator. On the doctors' advice, I signed a "do not resuscitate" order. That meant if Mom stopped breathing no extreme measures would be used to revive her. I was told the procedures probably wouldn't work and would only make a mess of her frail 90-year-old body.

But I was also concerned for Mom's spiritual health. We'd had many discussions about religion over the years. But still I wasn't totally sure where she was with God. Though she was heavily sedated, over the next two days I sat beside her and, now and then, I would talk to her about Him. I read her verses from His Word. I told her how much God loved her. I told her I wanted us to spend eternity together. I asked if she'd ever said yes to Yeshua, her Messiah. I was hoping I might get a flicker of response that would tell me she heard, comprehended, and believed.

What I got on a Tuesday afternoon, though, was a nurse yelling "code blue" in her room.

Mom's heart had stopped. I was quickly ushered out, and a hospital staff person pulled me into a waiting room. Someone asked what I wanted to do about the "do not resuscitate" order.

"I just want what's best for Mom, and I don't know what that is," I stammered.

God knew! He was about to do a miracle of restoration. One of the doctors thought one electric shock from a defibrillator might revive her. They tried it and it worked. Mom came back from the dead.

Now surgery was the only option if she was to survive. Unbelievably, she understood and agreed. She even made a scrawling attempt to sign the release form herself.

But that wasn't the greatest miracle. When I made a gentle inquiry about her spiritual state, Mom nodded "yes" to her acceptance of Yeshua.

Mom came through the surgery, but she didn't live many years more, as I'd hoped. She passed away just five-and-a-half months later. We did have some good times together though. We talked a bit more about spiritual things. And when she did pass through the door of death, I was left with the hope that we would indeed see each other again...in God's presence.

Two thousand years ago Jesus was urged to race to the side of a dying friend. He delayed, and Lazarus slipped away. His distraught family laid him in a tomb and mourned his loss. But Jesus knew what He was doing. He allowed Lazarus to die for a greater purpose. When He finally arrived in Lazarus' town, He went to the tomb and called His friend forth. And Lazarus came back from the dead! Not long after that Jesus died on a cross for the sins of the world and was raised from His tomb so we could all have resurrection hope in Him.

Tim and Lisa never dreamed they'd see Elsa again after all those months. I wasn't sure when Mom went "code blue" if I'd see her again in this life or in eternity. But the marvelous God we serve answered our prayers and worked His miracles of restoration. He who raised Lazarus and Jesus from the dead offers us resurrection hope. And He will surely work miracles of restoration in your life too—if you bring what seems lost before His throne and place your hope in Him.

And the God of all grace, who called you to his eternal glory in Christ, after you have suffered a little while, will himself restore you and make you strong, firm and steadfast (1 Peter 5:10).

Consider This

Have you seen God work a miracle of restoration in your life or in someone else's life? What was lost? What did God do? How did the situation grow your faith? How will this help you pray for and encourage others facing loss?

Pasha's Last Stand
God Shows Mercy in Miraculous Ways

*Where Mercy, Love and Pity dwell,
there God is dwelling too.*

WILLIAM BLAKE

Geoff was in college when the family dog, a spirited 12-year-old Afghan named Pasha, developed hip problems. He could hardly walk. Geoff feared the worst. He took Pasha to his apartment and looked after the dog to the best of his ability, but Pasha wasn't getting any better. Soon the dog could barely stand and the strength in his hind legs was gone. Pasha's quality of life had deteriorated to the point where Geoff was running out of options.

Heavyhearted, he contemplated taking Pasha to the vet for a final visit. Geoff looked into his dog's eyes and felt a surge of compassion. He got down on the floor, hugged Pasha close, and prayed. With childlike faith, Geoff asked God to have mercy on Pasha.

To Geoff's amazement, Pasha got up and walked as if nothing was wrong with him. It was a miracle!

For the next six months Pasha was a new dog. He regained his lively disposition and eager smile. He and Geoff took daily walks…and even went running a time or two. Geoff didn't take their time together for granted because he recognized the reprieve was a gift from God.

Then one day Pasha became completely listless. The vet said he couldn't find anything wrong with Pasha—only that his system was shutting down. That night Pasha passed away peacefully in his sleep.

Geoff doesn't remember Pasha with sadness. He is joyful that he was given an extra six months with his dog. The memories of them together will last a lifetime. But what affected Geoff the most was the mercy God showed the day he'd prayed for Pasha's healing. Geoff had no idea what God would do. He just put his hope in God's mercy…and God provided a miracle.

God has shown me mercy in miraculous ways too. Many years ago I used to wear hard contact lenses. When I woke up in the morning I had to wait at least an hour before I could comfortably insert the "foreign objects" into my eyes. If I didn't get enough sleep or give my eyes time to "wake up," the lenses would feel dry and gritty all day. Since I was a "late to bed, late to rise" kind of guy, I grabbed every moment of sleep I could. That meant having a half hour, at best, to get ready for work. To delay putting in my contacts, I often wore glasses on the drive to my job. When I arrived, I parked and carefully put in my contacts while sitting behind the wheel. Then I got out and walked to the office building.

One day during this ritual a lens slipped off my finger. I searched my shirt and pants for the wayward bit of glass, but it hid itself well. I scoured my car seat and rug. I panicked. I was almost blind in one eye, and I couldn't find that lens! And I was going to be late for work. Giving up the search, I rushed the two blocks to my office, ran up the stairs to my desk, and with great visual irritation somehow made it through the day.

Back home I took the car seats out and with a powerful utility lamp obsessively searched for the missing lens. I combed every inch of my '66 Mustang's carpet. I checked every nook and cranny. No luck! The lens was gone. Fortunately I had an extra one. Unfortunately it was scratched. After a few hours of wearing it, my eye would sting. I put up with this situation for two weeks, but I finally realized I'd have to make an appointment with my optometrist. I hated to miss work to go and didn't want to spend the money.

One morning I got so angry on my way to work that when I put in that scratchy lens and felt it sting, I railed at God. Logically it wasn't His fault I'd lost my contact. I knew that. But if He truly is so hands-on that He knows every hair of my head and faithfully feeds and cares for the birds of the field, why didn't He step in and keep me from losing the lens...or at least help me find it? As I trudged the two blocks to work, walked up the three flights of stairs, and headed for my office, I looked up and told God that my eye really was hurting. I knew it wasn't a life-or-death situation, but my soul cried out to Him for mercy. Once in my office, I let out a sigh of exasperation and looked down at my desk—a desk wiped clean of everything...except for a small, shiny object lying in the middle of the dark, wood-veneered surface.

No! It couldn't be! I picked it up. It was a lens—a hard contact lens. I did what eye doctors say never to do. I put some spit on it and stuck it into my eye. It was a perfect fit. It was my lens!

I've come up with two possible explanations: 1) God made that lens materialize on my desk, or 2) when the lens first dropped out of my eye, it fell on my shirt, stuck on me for the two-block walk and three-flights-of-stairs climb, and fell off me in my office. Maybe it sat tight where it was for a couple of weeks until a kindly janitor spied it, picked it up, and put it on my desk for me to see... which just happened to occur on the very day, at the very moment

I cried out to God, spotted the lens, and recognized its return as a manifestation of His mercy. Either way, getting my lens back was a miracle from God!

Just as God answered Geoff's cry for mercy and miraculously healed Pasha, in His beautifully quirky, creative way, God had mercy on me and restored my sight.

And He has been doing the same thing for the blind and hard-of-seeing for a long, long time—so we can see His love more clearly.

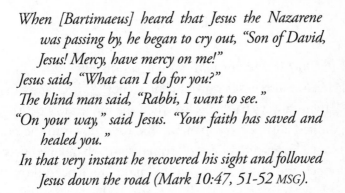

> When [Bartimaeus] heard that Jesus the Nazarene was passing by, he began to cry out, "Son of David, Jesus! Mercy, have mercy on me!"
> Jesus said, "What can I do for you?"
> The blind man said, "Rabbi, I want to see."
> "On your way," said Jesus. "Your faith has saved and healed you."
> In that very instant he recovered his sight and followed Jesus down the road (Mark 10:47, 51-52 MSG).

Consider This

How have you seen God's mercy and miracles in your life? In other people's lives? How did it impact your faith?

The Heart of the Father
God Is Love

*Father!—to God himself we cannot
give a holier name.*

WILLIAM WORDSWORTH

Kim Dorr is a pastor with an entertainment ministry in Los Angeles. She also has her own talent agency. As a kid growing up, her parents always had dogs, so when she moved to Los Angeles, she wanted a canine companion. She went down to the pound and looked over the dozens of orphans and abandoned pets. As Kim knelt and put her hand on the chain link fence, all the dogs backed away except one. The little German shepherd/husky puppy licked her hand. They took him home that day and christened him Jachomo.

Jachomo was special. He was the first dog Kim owned as an adult, and they bonded closely.

Around 12 years of age, Jachomo developed an almost imperceptible limp. Gradually he lost the use of his hind legs and his ability to "do his business" by himself. Kim did everything she could to avoid the inevitable, but finally her close friends told her she needed to put her beloved dog down.

Kim took Jachomo to the vet, and she still remembers it feeling like an out-of-body experience as she watched her hand signing her name on the required paper giving the vet permission to euthanize her pet. She got down on the floor next to Jachomo and let him rest his head on her lap. The nurse shaved his front leg as the vet readied the injection. Kim couldn't watch and turned her face away, all the while holding Jachomo in her arms, gently petting him, tears streaming down her face. After a few moments, Kim turned her eyes toward the nurse and asked, "How long does this take?" The nurse softly told her Jachomo was already gone. Kim's heart broke and she wept uncontrollably.

This took place a few weeks before Easter. Shortly afterward, Kim was driving in her car, still raw from the loss of her precious companion. She was listening to a sermon on the radio. A pastor was discussing Jesus' death on the cross. Kim had a mental flashback of holding Jachomo in her arms as he passed from life to death. As she pondered her own pain and what happened on the cross, she felt a new and special bond with the heart of the Father. While Jesus was completely human and knew our deepest pains, sorrows, joys, and temptations, she realized in a new way that the first person of the Trinity—way up in heaven, invisible and omnipresent—is not a detached, cold, and unfeeling being. He's a loving, caring Father.

Kim reflected that we often focus on the pain Jesus endured on the cross. Perhaps we need to consider the agony it cost the Father to send His Son to live as a human and be offered up for us. As painful as it had been to lose Jachomo, her treasured pet of 12 years, what must it have cost the Father to watch His beloved Son die on the cross, knowing that it was part of His plan, sovereignly ordained from the foundation of the world? Doing what is best doesn't minimize the loss or the suffering experienced as a result.

"Contemplating the heart of the Father—what He endured for me, what He gave up for me—drew me much closer into the fullness of the heart of God," Kim says. "The life of Jesus became even more precious to me as I stood side-by-side with the Father in my mind and envisioned His pain. From this insight I gained a new awareness of how to speak of the Father's love for His children… for you and me. And when Easter morning came that year, the victory over the grave was much more exhilarating—more vibrantly alive in my heart. The joy of the Father's loving fellowship with the Son and the Son's loving fellowship with the Father has been restored. That is the joy we are ushered into in Christ."

Praise be to the God and Father of our Lord Jesus Christ, the Father of compassion and the God of all comfort, who comforts us in all our troubles, so that we can comfort those in any trouble with the comfort we ourselves have received from God (2 Corinthians 1:3-4).

Consider This

Have you lost someone you deeply loved? What was that experience like? What insights does it give you into God the Father's heart when His Son died on the cross for us?

Is your relationship with your earthly father close and loving? Or is it more distant? How has that affected your relationship with your heavenly Father?

A Reason to Dance
With All You Are, Praise God

You can dance anywhere, even if only in your heart.
AUTHOR UNKNOWN

My dogs dance. It's a trick I taught them. Biscuit rises high on her hind legs and twirls. Morgan used to perform a more wobbly turn, but now that he's older and has some back problems he "dances" by walking in a circle. Becca spins rapidly on the ground and sometimes lifts her front paws as she does so. Though my dogs' styles vary, they all dance for the very same reason. They want the tasty treat they know it will earn them. That is good enough motivation that sometimes they'll even initiate dancing on their own to see if they can trigger a treat when they choose.

Lately I've been watching some dance competitions on television. These contests also offer rewards. On one show, couples compete for a large trophy and bragging rights. On another, dancers vie for a huge cash prize. Even those who don't win the top "treat" get other rewards, such as new friendships and the new steps and experiences they've encountered that might help improve their lives and careers. All of these are good reasons to dance.

None of them are Jessica's.

Jessica is my favorite dancer. She isn't on those dancing shows. She isn't even on her feet. Jessica is 12, and she's afflicted with cerebral palsy. She dances in her wheelchair.

I met Jessica through her mother. She specializes in plant care, and she's worked for my family for years. Recently she showed me a DVD of Jessica dancing with her teacher. The young girl was a beautiful portrait of joy in motion. Jessica danced with her arms and wheelchair gracefully moving in time to the music as she propelled herself across the floor and in circles. Jessica's teacher twirled her arms and body in a fluid duet with her pupil.

I've seen some marvelous choreography on those dance shows, but this touched my heart so much more. Jessica's dance made my heart leap at the endless possibilities of an indomitable spirit. It proved creative expression can soar despite life's challenges. I was reminded that we all have the potential to create because we've been made in the image of our great Creator God.

Jessica's dance also held a mirror up to my attitudes toward life. I realized I sometimes let such small things get me down. If I gain a pound, I'm bummed. If I'm struggling with a story, I wonder about my abilities as a writer. But this little girl in a wheelchair—whose challenges are far greater than mine—reaches out to embrace every opportunity life offers her, including dancing with joy. What greater delight might I experience if I approach life like she does?

Yes, I got so much out of Jessica's dance. But what did she get? What was her reason for dancing? I didn't want to assume, so I asked her mom. I learned that Jessica loves to dance because she thinks it's fun. It also shows her she can do what other kids can do. I loved hearing that because I believe God wants all of us to dance...in praise of Him.

I don't know precisely what Jessica believes about God, but I know what God's Word says about dance.

> Let Israel rejoice in their Maker; let the people of Zion be glad in their King. Let them praise his name with dancing and make music to him with tambourine and harp. For the LORD takes delight in his people; he crowns the humble with salvation. Let the saints rejoice in this honor and sing for joy on their beds (Psalm 149:2-5).

God doesn't say, "Let only the skilled dance." He doesn't ask just His able-bodied children to do so. He doesn't say, "Hold a contest and choose only the best dancers to perform for Me." He doesn't dangle a treat in the air to coax our obedience to His commands like I do with my dogs. He simply tells us to dance in praise and worship of Him.

Does this mean that we must incorporate dance in our worship? No, I don't think so. What I think, in a broader sense, is that we are to use the creativity He gives us to praise and honor Him. Regardless of our ages or health or talents or circumstances, we are to celebrate Him. If we are delighting in Him, He will take enormous pleasure in us.

In my life, dancing in praise of God means flowing, rhythmic words twirling across pages and computer screens. I love creating images that dance in people's minds. I illustrate how God works in my life and in the lives of others. And because I love to sing, I also "dance in song" to the Lord by singing praise songs at church. I don't have a very melodic voice, but I sing aloud, blissfully drowned out by those around me. I know God loves my heart of worship.

As I mentioned, I taught my dogs to dance. But Morgan learned one move all on his own. Sometimes he spontaneously leaps into the air. Perhaps it's something in his genes, but I think of it as his "happy dance," an expression of his joy. It's his way of bursting with love for his life and his master, and it delights my heart.

And you know what? Sometimes when I'm thrilled at something the Lord has done, I leap into the air and shout for joy. I believe this delights my Master too. It pleases Him when I praise Him with my whole being. Isn't this the best reason of all to dance?

You turned my wailing into dancing; you removed my sackcloth and clothed me with joy, that my heart may sing to you and not be silent. O LORD my God, I will give you thanks forever (Psalm 30:11-12).

Consider This

What are some ways you express yourself creatively? How can you use these in worshiping the Lord? How can you join your creative gifts with the gifts of others to praise God and bring Him glory?

Doggie in the Window
Watch for the Master

*Having someone wonder where you are when
you don't come home at night
is a very old human need.*

MARGARET MEAD

When my wife's niece Priscilla came home from work in the evening, it warmed her heart to see her joyful Pomeranian, Brownie, waiting eagerly for her. Brownie would be standing on the couch looking out the living room window. Priscilla's new roommate told her Brownie dashed to her watch post even before her master was in sight—most likely hearing the distinct drone of Priscilla's car.

What Priscilla didn't know until her roommate told her was what Brownie did when her master left for work in the morning. The loyal dog jumped on the couch and watched Priscilla drive away, not budging until the car was gone from view.

Priscilla was touched. She murmured a long "awwwwww" as she scooped Brownie into her arms and smothered her baby with hugs and kisses. Knowing her little dog loved and worshiped her lifted Priscilla's spirits even when she'd had a bad day at work or it seemed everything was going wrong. Coming home to her faithful "doggie in the window" always put a smile on her face and in her heart.

Sadly, we humans don't always do as good a job as our dogs do when it comes to making our loved ones feel cared about and wanted. My wife often bears the brunt of this. There have been times when I'm busy writing on my computer, absorbed in worlds of my own creation, inhabiting the psyches of strange and shadowy characters. Our son, Skye, is on his computer, putting his pedal to the video metal as his cyber race car speeds past a rival at 200 miles per hour. If Celine, my wife and Skye's mom, arrives home from her day at such moments, she isn't greeted by people watching eagerly for her return. She walks into an empty living room. The only hug awaiting her is from an armchair. She calls our names and often doesn't even get an echo back. Only after playing an unwanted game of search-and-find through the house does she finally come upon us, our faces glazed over as we sit in the glow of our computer screens. When her exasperated sigh grabs our attention at last, we look up to see her hurt expression that says, "You don't love me."

Thankfully our family believes in forgiveness and second chances. We move on and purpose to do better next time. Disappointing someone we love occasionally happens. We're distracted. We're self-centered. We tend to put our own interests first. But our loved ones need visible signs of our care and adoration. Simple gestures, such as watching at the window, can communicate so much!

In God's Word, Jesus tells us He will return at a time we might not expect. He says, "Keep watch, because you do not know on what day your Lord will come" (Matthew 24:42).

Just as it delighted Priscilla to find Brownie waiting for her, just as Celine longs to see Skye and me excitedly welcoming her home, so our loving Master in heaven desires to see us eagerly watching and waiting for Him. What does this look like in real life? How do we look out the window for God?

We can keep our hearts and minds firmly fixed on Jesus. A wise person once told me to do four things daily to stay close to God and grow in my relationship with Him: worship, pray, read His Word, and spend time in fellowship with other believers. These four things are like standing at the window, demonstrating our love and devotion for God.

If these four things were one-way windows into the heavenly realms, how often and for how long each day would God see your joyful face peering out, watching longingly and lovingly for Him?

Be dressed ready for service and keep your lamps burning, like men waiting for their master to return from a wedding banquet, so that when he comes and knocks they can immediately open the door for him. It will be good for those servants whose master finds them watching when he comes (Luke 12:35-37).

Consider This

Are you watching eagerly for your Master? If not, what things are distracting you? What do you need to do to change this? What are some creative ways you can show your love and devotion to God?

Forever Family
God's Adoptions Are Final

*The happiest moments of my life have
been the few which I have passed at
home in the bosom of my family.*

THOMAS JEFFERSOM

My uncle's family used to say if their West Highland terrier, Katie, was a human, she'd be running IBM. She was as sweet as she was smart, and they adored her. So when she died a tragic and untimely death, they wanted to adopt another "Westie"— preferably a rescue.

After some searching, they found the perfect pup. She was with a rescue group in another state. Unfortunately, when they contacted the agency and asked about the little orphan, her guardians balked. They didn't like out-of-state adoptions because they'd had a bad experience with one. A family had gotten a dog and then wanted to give it back. Retrieving the pup from a distance had been difficult and costly. The rescue agency didn't want to go through that kind of situation again.

My uncle's family insisted they would never do this. They backed it up by providing sterling references. In the end, the rescue group relented. My relatives welcomed their new "Katie" and have loved and adored her ever since. They wouldn't dream of parting with her. She is in her "forever family."

Another orphan also found a forever family. Raina was adopted some years ago by my friends Tom and Annie. She had to cross an ocean to join her new parents. In the country where she was born, a child could be left at an orphanage for several months and then reclaimed with no questions asked. When Raina's relatives left her they said they'd be back for her. They never returned.

Raina was put up for adoption and suffered even more abandonment. She was taken home by prospective new parents, only to be returned. Fortunately Tom and Annie decided to adopt after failing to conceive a child. They found Raina's photograph on the internet and fell in love. Adopting Raina was complicated. My friends made multiple trips overseas. They jumped through endless administrative hoops. They filled out reams of paperwork. Finally the young girl was released to them. They flew to her country, picked her up, and returned home to the United States to begin their new lives as a family.

Unlike Katie (the dog), Raina's adjustment was far from smooth. Tom and Annie knew she was theirs forever...but Raina didn't. Her past traumas made her fear she would be deserted again. She especially bonded with Annie, so if Annie left her, she screamed and threw tantrums in terror.

Tom and Annie's faith in God was strong. They trust in Jesus as their Savior and Lord, so they prayed about this adoption long and hard. And they had no doubt whatsoever that God had given them this child. Lovingly, patiently, prayerfully, they set about helping her adjust and discover that, at last, she had parents who would not forsake her. Gradually, as they proved their faithfulness, Raina's confidence and security grew. Today she's a happy, well-adjusted, outgoing young lady because she knows that whatever happens, her parents are there for her.

Not every rescue dog finds a home. And not every human orphan does either. Sadly, not all parents are faithful as Tom and Annie are. But each of us has a standing offer of adoption by our heavenly Father who pledges He will never abandon His children. And He always keeps His promises! In John 1:12-13 we read, "Yet to all who received [Jesus], to those who believed in his name, he gave the right to become children of God—children born not of natural descent, nor of human decision or a husband's will, but born of God." And Psalm 9:10 assures us, "Those who know your name will trust in you, for you, LORD, have never forsaken those who seek you."

God understands the past hurts you've suffered. He understands that if you've been abandoned, it may take you some time to trust Him wholeheartedly. He is loving and patient, willing to prove His faithfulness. So let Him welcome you into His "forever family" so you can rest securely in the arms of the God who will never let you go.

Though my father and mother forsake me, the LORD will receive me (Psalm 27:10).

Consider This

Do you struggle with abandonment fears? What past hurts contributed to this? How have they affected your ability to trust God? How is God working in your life to reveal His faithfulness?

When You Chase a Car...
Motives Matter

*In all our actions, God considers the intention:
whether we act for Him or for some other motive.*

St. Maximus the Confessor

Eric grew up in the Wisconsin countryside amid lots of wide-open spaces and dairy farms. He lived five miles from the nearest school. As a ten-year-old, he walked out of his house each morning with his trusty collie/spaniel mix, Sailor, and waited for the school bus. Sailor always stood by Eric until he was safely aboard and watched until the bright-yellow vehicle disappeared. Then Sailor would return to his yard. He was a very loyal and protective dog.

One day Eric was late...or, as he tells it, the bus left early. He was stranded. Thankfully, a neighbor noticed his predicament and offered him a ride to school. Eric gladly accepted.

This did not sit right with Sailor! Eric wasn't getting on the familiar yellow school bus. No, he was getting into a strange, much smaller, dark-colored automobile. As Eric waved goodbye and shut the door, Sailor barked hysterically. When the car drove off, Eric glanced back to see Sailor running after the car. Sailor ran his heart out up and down the twisting country roads, following for over a mile and a half. Eric couldn't believe it as he watched Sailor vanish from view. He worried whether his loyal friend would find his way home.

Sailor did. When Eric got home from school that afternoon, he found his dog waiting for him, tail wagging as usual. Eric didn't scold his dog for foolishly chasing a car and risking getting lost or hit by another car. He wasn't angry with Sailor. Instead he felt great appreciation. Eric realized that Sailor's actions, although misguided, were motivated by his love for his young master.

Motives matter with children too. My wife, Celine, keeps two piles of paper by her printer. One is the recycle pile—paper used on one side. She uses the plain side to print less important items. The other is the new pile—unused paper she reserves for formal documents. When our then-six-year-old son, Skye, wanted to practice his artistic skills, Celine instructed him to use only the "recycled" paper. She didn't want to waste new paper on crayon drawings.

One day she "caught" Skye hunkered down on the hardwood floor, scribbling on a sheet of clean, unused paper. A flare of indignation rose. "Never use new paper for your drawings!" she admonished as she reached for the page.

The little boy looked up and countered, "But I'm making a card for Daddy!"

Celine took a closer look at the card. It had funny faces with bugged-out eyes and stuck-out tongues, a shark baring its teeth, and a dinosaur. It also was illustrated with VW car logos Skye enjoyed drawing. In the midst of all the art, in huge green letters, were the words "HAPPY BIRTHDAY DADDY!"

Celine couldn't resist smiling. She understood the motive behind Skye's disobedience, and she was totally disarmed. Like Sailor, Skye was acting out of love. She gave the paper back to him and told him to keep drawing. She said it was a beautiful card, and she knew his daddy would appreciate it.

In our relationship with God, the attitude of our hearts—that oftentimes only He can truly know and see—is also more important than our actions. When Jesus' disciples were indignant that a woman poured expensive perfume over Him, lamenting that it could have been sold to provide cash for the poor, Jesus replied,

> Why are you bothering this woman? She has done a beautiful thing to me. The poor you will always have with you, but you will not always have me. When she poured this perfume on my body, she did it to prepare me for burial (Matthew 26:10-12).

Eric appreciated Sailor's "foolish" car chase. Celine and I appreciated Skye's "extravagant" use of new paper. And Jesus appreciated a woman's "wasteful" pouring of expensive perfume. If we take time to look beyond people's actions, discover the positive motives of their hearts, and observe them through eyes of love, we'll experience many blessings.

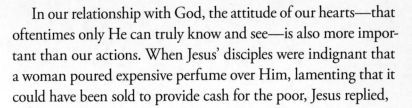

GOD examines every heart and sees through every motive (1 Chronicles 28:9 MSG).

Consider This

Have you ever condemned someone's actions because you didn't understand his or her motive? When you learned the true intent, what effect did it have on your attitude? Has anyone misjudged your actions?

Special Places
Do You Have a Special Prayer Spot?

Come near to God and
he will come near to you.

JAMES 4:8

My dogs love having a stay-at-home mom. Since I'm a writer and work from the house, they get to hang out with me all day. Even so, Morgan wants more. He has staked out some special spots where he can cuddle and commune with me, and he isn't shy about asking for private time with me.

One of those places is my office easy chair. The instant I lean back and pop up the footrest, he knows. That's his signal to trot over and jump up beside me. He swings his little body around and nestles down between my outstretched legs and the chair's side. There he lies, eyes closed, contentedly basking in my presence. Even if another dog or cat beats him into the chair, which sometimes happens, he still squeezes himself into his favored spot. He is willing to endure another pet lying half on top of him rather than relinquish his preferred place next to me.

Morgan also likes to have some lap time when I'm at my

computer. He asks for this by putting his paws up on me. I lift him up and he snuggles until he's ready to jump down or I need to put him back on the floor and get to work.

There are other spots in the house where Morgan comes to be close to me. He lies beneath a bar stool in the kitchen while I drink my morning coffee. When I watch TV, he curls up next to me on the den couch. All the dogs sleep with me at night, but Morgan sometimes drapes his warm, furry body across my legs. I delight in all these sweet expressions of his love and devotion and desire to be with me.

I also have some special places where I commune with my Master. One of these is my walking route. I walk an hour a day on the hilly streets near my home. Other than occasional meetings with neighbors, I'm usually alone in this lovely setting. It's a wonderful time to be with the Lord. I pray about my needs and the needs of others. I talk with the Lord about stories I'm writing. As I walk and meditate, He gives me fresh ideas and connections I can add to my work when I get back home.

In years past, I met with the Lord while in a pool. I swam for exercise for long stretches of time. It was a peaceful, solitary place to speak to God and listen to Him speak to me.

Most of us have special spots where we meet with God. I always enjoy hearing about someone else's favored location. My friend Vicenta has a wonderfully creative prayer place. She was inspired by a suggestion that when praying for someone it might be helpful to be looking at his or her picture. She took this concept to the next level by creating a photo prayer wall next to the desk where she regularly studies God's Word. She's had as many as 25 photos posted at once. She puts up pictures of her large family, photos of people her children are dating, and people who have asked for special prayer requests. Others who know about Vicenta's wall and want prayer for friends and family contribute pictures to be posted too.

Another special place and time Vicenta meets God is in bed early in the morning. She says it's one of the few times she's awake and still. God once woke her up at four thirty, urging her to have a significant prayer time before rising to dive into her busy day.

Morgan's time with me isn't limited to his special spots, but spending time there together builds our closeness. And though God is always with us, having special places and times to meet Him helps draw us into a deeper relationship with Him. I delight in Morgan's desire to have these special tête-a-têtes with me. How much more must our desire for God cause Him to take delight in us!

Very early in the morning, while it was still dark, Jesus got up, left the house and went off to a solitary place, where he prayed (Mark 1:35).

Consider This

Do you have a special place where you pray and spend time with God? Why did you choose that spot? What about it helps you commune with Him? What difference has this made in your spiritual life? If you don't have such a place, where might you establish one?

Trespassing...or Not?
Love Knows No Barriers

*No law or ordinance is mightier
than understanding.*

PLATO

The Lee family's white lab, Sam, knew Susu was pregnant before she did. He'd been constantly sniffing her for weeks. Susu, with her kooky sense of humor, thought Sam's attention strangely flattering until she found out she was expecting their third child. Then it all made sense. For the rest of the pregnancy, Sam continued to sniff her and show great curiosity about what was happening.

The day Susu and her husband, Eric, brought Gabriella home from the hospital, they put her in a bassinet in their bedroom. Sam was in the kitchen—the only place in the house where he was allowed. There wasn't a fence or a "do not trespass" sign written in dog language. He just stayed true to his training and kept in his area. So when Eric and Susu returned from the bedroom and saw Sam toeing the boundary between the kitchen and living room, they noticed. The anxious dog looked up at his masters, who were waiting to see what their well-trained and obedient pet would do.

There was an internal drumroll as Sam crossed the forbidden line and moved past his open-mouthed masters. He went straight into the bedroom and gazed at the newborn baby in the bassinet. Eric and Susu were awed. It was easy to see Sam adored the child. To this day, Sam and Gabriella have a special bond. Sam's love for Gabriella knew no boundaries or law.

Like with Sam, there have been times when certain laws didn't make sense to me. When I was a kid, I took a road trip with my uncle from California to Mississippi. One day we stopped at a restaurant in the Deep South to grab a bite to eat. I went to the restroom by myself, but hesitated when I saw a sign that said: "White Men Only." I looked around and saw another sign with an arrow pointing around to the back. It read: "Colored Restrooms."

Being an obedient Chinese-American child, I hesitated. Both signs were professionally painted, so this was obviously an accepted "law" in these parts. I knew this was a black/white issue, but being of Asian descent, I also knew Chinese were often referred to as "yellow." And yellow wasn't white. Therefore, logically, maybe I was supposed to use the restrooms for "colored" people.

But something inside told me this law wasn't right. It was not what I'd learned in school. I'd been taught that all people were created equal. So I went into the "White Men Only" restroom. As far as I know, no one saw me or realized the dilemma I faced and my solution. The entire conflict played out in my mind. I sensed a higher "law" that superseded the intent behind the sign on that door. Even as a kid I knew in my heart that whether we were black, white, or yellow, we were all God's children. And God didn't put up those kinds of barriers!

Isn't it amazing that our entire relationship with God and our gift of eternal life hinges on Someone who more than 2000 years ago refused to obey many signs, rules, and regulations made by the "high and mighty" lawmakers of His day? Jesus crossed the line and defied human restraints to dine with tax collectors, associate with Samaritans, and heal people on the Sabbath. He even allowed His disciples to pick and eat grain on the Sabbath. To the Pharisees, who had reinterpreted God's law for their own self-serving purposes, Jesus was a blasphemous rule-breaker deserving of death. But in the eyes of His Father, Jesus was sinless and the perfect fulfillment of the law.

Today Gabriella feels honored every time she hears the story of how Sam crossed the human-set line out of love for her. And we too are also honored—and humbled—that Jesus crossed the line out of His love for us. The sign on Christ's door says "There is neither Jew nor Greek, slave nor free, male nor female, for you all are one in Christ Jesus" (Galatians 3:28). There are no barriers in God's family. We are one in His sight and love forever!

"Love the Lord your God with all your heart and with all your soul and with all your mind." This is the first and greatest commandment. And the second is like it: "Love your neighbor as yourself." All the Law and the Prophets hang on these two commandments (Matthew 22:37-40).

Consider This

Have you had to deal with laws that put barriers between you and others? Did you obey them or defy them? Was your choice the right thing in God's sight?

Will the Real "Dog Mom" Please Stand Up?

The Proof Is in the Caring

Simply having children does not make mothers.

JOHN A. SHEDD

Mom had three dogs, but my favorite was her Pomeranian named Bebe. After Mom's death, Bebe came to live with me. I renamed her Becca and worked on getting her to bond with me as her new "dog mom."

Becca is an adventurous gal. Given the chance, she'll bolt. One day after I let her and my other two dogs out in the yard to do their business, I saw to my horror that the back gate was open. I quickly looked for Becca. She'd vanished! I ran to the street. A close friend had just driven up with his daughter. Sabrina had already spied Becca on the sidewalk and scooped her up.

This young lady and her family know my dogs and cats well. They often care for them when I go out of town. Sabrina loves all of them, but she's developed a special affection for Becca. A few days after the gate incident, Sabrina and I were talking about how she'd saved Becca. Sabrina commented, "That proves I'm her mom, right?"

I'm ashamed to say I got a bit jealous of this little girl's relationship with my dog. My first insecure, emotional response was, "No, I'm her mom. You're her auntie. And we need to be careful she doesn't get confused about that."

Looking back, I think my guts were playing an "old tape" recorded in my childhood. I was unpopular as a kid and developed low self-esteem. I always thought someone else would get picked over me. That fear of being the one "not chosen" carried over to my relationship with pets. In my twenties I shared an apartment with a housemate. We each had a cat. Soon my cat didn't want to sleep with me at night anymore. He preferred to curl up with my friend and her kitty. It drove me nuts. I kept going and getting him so he'd be in my bedroom with me. But those kinds of things can't be forced...especially with cats. My fickle pet would slip back into my roommate's room the first chance he got. I felt totally rejected.

Now I was having similar feelings. I was afraid my new dog would pick Sabrina over me. But looking back, the very reason Sabrina claimed "motherhood" should have told me things would be just fine. The true mark of a parent isn't giving birth to or owning a "child." The essence of motherhood is loving, protecting, and caring for the youngster in question. This girl adored my dog, and Becca sensed and responded to her feelings. Over the long haul, I'd be doing much more mothering—and my new dog would figure this out and know who her "main mom" is.

I knew this because that's exactly what happened to my friend Maxine (Max). She and her husband, John, weren't able to conceive and had decided against fertility treatments. They wanted children to love, so they adopted a baby boy from Korea. When he was three, they adopted a sister for him from the same country.

Though they'd traveled to Korea to get Kevin, they decided that with a toddler, they'd have their new daughter flown to the United States with an escort. When the time came, I accompanied Max and John to the airport to welcome Karin to her new home.

When Karin was in the foster home in Korea, she apparently bonded best with men. And now she wanted nothing to do with her new mom. She let John hold her but would scream the moment Max tried to take her. Fortunately Max wasn't bothered or threatened like I'd been with Becca. She just chuckled. She knew she'd win this child over.

During the next weeks and months, Max cemented her maternal relationship with her new baby girl. Karin quickly grew to adore her mother.

Even when Max had to discipline her bright and often headstrong daughter, she showed her mother's heart to Karin in the process. Once when Karin was acting up in public, I heard Max explain that if she behaved this way, her friends' parents might not enjoy having her visit at their houses. She should learn to act in a way that would make her a welcomed guest so she could have fun with her friends. Karin got the message and was thankful, in her little-girl way, for her mother's loving discipline.

When they were old enough, Max explained to both children that they were adopted. She and John had decided that the details of their family wouldn't be hidden. She made it very clear to them that in every way that mattered she was their mommy and John was their daddy. She emphasized that she and John loved them completely, and that to them both kids were their own and part of them in every way.

Sadly, Max didn't live long enough to raise her beloved children to adulthood. One day when Karin was 13, Max suffered a heart attack or stroke. She passed away at the young age of 50. When both kids were offered counseling, they declined. They told me, their "auntie," later that they'd had such a fabulous mom they didn't think anyone else could fully comprehend the magnitude of their loss. And they still had their dad to help them through the difficult time.

Just as Max proved her claim to be a mom by her love and caring, God proves His loving Fatherhood by His great love for us. He sent Jesus to die for us so we could be adopted into His family for eternity. He gives us His ongoing care and blessings forever if we will simply accept the forgiveness He offers through faith in Christ and choose Him as our Lord and Savior. Our all-wise Father knows what I had to learn: Real love can't be forced. He lets us choose how we will respond to Him.

These days Becca still loves Sabrina. I've conferred on her the title "honorary dog mom." My dog knows her real "mom" is me. Becca sleeps on my bed at night, races to me when I call her, and covers me quickly with doggie kisses. My love has won her heart, and she's mine totally—just as God's love has won me, and I am His totally.

The apostle Paul understood the power of God's love. In Ephesians 3:17-19, he wrote,

> I pray that you, being rooted and established in love, may have power, together with all the saints, to grasp how wide and long and high and deep is the love of Christ, and to know this love that surpasses knowledge—that you may be filled to the measure of all the fullness of God.

God the Father wants you to join His family as a full and complete member. He waits with arms outstretched to welcome you home. Run to Him! Bask in His eternal love!

When the time had fully come, God sent his Son, born of a woman, born under law, to redeem those under law, that we might receive the full rights of sons. Because you are sons [and daughters], God sent the Spirit of his Son into our hearts, the Spirit who calls out, "Abba, Father." So you are no longer a slave, but a son [or daughter]; and since you are a son [or daughter], God has made you also an heir (Galatians 4:4-7).

Consider This

Have you been adopted into God's family? If yes, what are some ways He shows you His love? How has this drawn you closer to Him as your Father?

If you haven't chosen to run into God's arms as His child forever, what is holding you back?

Two Are Better Than One
God Made Us to Be in Relationship

*People are lonely because they
build walls instead of bridges.*

JOSEPH FORT NEWTON

I was stressed as I drove home. Company was coming for dinner, and I wasn't ready. I'd had a hard day substitute teaching, my arthritis was acting up, and I didn't feel like being a gracious host. But when I walked through my back door, I heard the doggie door open and close. Squitchey, my family's sweet, "bad hair day" dog, raced up to greet me. By the time the guests came, I was renewed in spirit and ready to enjoy the evening.

Squitchey makes life better for everyone she meets. She loves greeting our guests and can't wait for the door to open so she can enthusiastically meet them. Once they've seen her, she jumps onto the back of Steve's easy chair so she can look at them face-to-face. Her antics make people smile.

My mom loved Squitchey. When she visited us, she always invited Squitchey to sit beside her on the sofa or next to her on the floor. The amiable dog made Mom happy just by being there, and being needed made Squitchey happy. Our littlest dog is a beautiful illustration of what being in relationship can add to our lives.

Just as Squitchey has enriched our home, a very special little girl named Mia has enriched the lives of the people at Disneyland. She goes to Disneyland almost every week. Mia was born with Down syndrome. Her life is filled with challenges, but she diligently works hard to overcome them with the help of her mom and dad. When her parents, Alicia and Danny, enrolled Mia in kindergarten, she exceeded all the goals set for her. The other children accepted and loved her. The biggest problem was that Mia was frightened by loud noises. Alicia's cousin Herb bought Disneyland season tickets for Mia and her parents, hoping that visiting the joyfully noisy "happiest place on earth" would help her adjust to the cacophony.

Their first visit was difficult. Mia panicked on the tram ride from the parking lot to the park. Danny held her in his arms as she hid her face in his neck. Alicia tried to reassure her, telling her that yes, there were a lot of people, but everything was going to be all right. Mia didn't believe her. They repeated the trip, and over the next few months she began to realize it was true and that everything was going to be okay.

Going to Disneyland week after week, Mia soon formed relationships with the Disneyland staff. When Mia goes through the Disneyland gates, they greet her with smiles, hugs, and enthusiastic hellos. She has her own name tag, and many of the Disney employees consider her part of their "family." Cast members holler, "Hi, Mia!" as they march by in parade. When the "Trash Can Trio," a percussion group in the park, knows Mia is visiting, they bring her a can and mallet so she can make music with them. This delights Mia and many of the other guests.

When Mia's parents thanked the Disneyland staff membsers,

they said they were thankful for Mia too. One Disney worker, Alyssa, made Mia a scrapbook that included pages and pages of pictures and notes from Disneyland cast members. The short letters reveal sweet stories of how Mia so positively affected their lives.

Because of her Disney experiences, Mia has outgrown her fear of loud noises and crowds and does much better in school.

Isn't it wonderful how pets and other people help us get more enjoyment out of life? God created us to worship Him. And He also built within us the need for relationships. Ecclesiastes 4:9 says, "Two are better than one, because they have a good return for their work." In our home there's a good return—happiness—when Squitchey is in the mix. At Disneyland, there's a good return—joy—when Mia visits. When we embrace the relationships with people and animals God puts in our lives, we're blessed…and hopefully we're blessing them too!

Be devoted to one another in brotherly love. Honor one another above yourselves (Romans 12:10).

Consider This

What is the most special relationship in your life? How has it revealed that "two are better than one"? What are some of the "good returns" it has provided? Is there a relationship you're shying away from that God may want to use to bless both of you?

A Capful of Hope
God's Promises Never Fail

*Hope is faith holding out its
hand in the dark.*

GEORGE ILES

When Carl was 15, he went ice skating early one Saturday morning on a frozen pond not far from his house. His collie, Penny, trailed eagerly after him, her white-and-sable fur glistening in the cold morning sun. While Carl was zipping around on the pond, Penny wandered off. Unfortunately she wasn't as discerning as Carl about which areas of the pond had ice thick enough to romp on.

Suddenly Carl heard a splash. He looked over and saw that Penny had fallen through the ice. Only her head was sticking out of the freezing water as she frantically tried to pull herself up on the ice. Carl skated over but he couldn't pull Penny free. He panicked. The pond wasn't deep enough for his dog to drown, but he knew she would soon freeze to death. Penny was depending on him. What should he do?

Carl decided to race home and get his dad. He told Penny to hang on and that he'd be right back. When he saw the fear in his dog's eyes, Carl pulled off his wool cap, held it out for Penny to smell, and placed it on the ice in front of her face. Carl gave Penny a pat on the head and promised once more that he would return. He hoped that while he was away his cap would comfort Penny and reassure her that he wasn't abandoning her.

Carl ran home and returned with his father. They pulled a shivering, grateful Penny out of the pond. As his dad loaded Penny into the car and wrapped a towel around her, Carl retrieved his wool cap. Penny didn't need it anymore. She'd received the fulfillment of the promise. She was taken home, dried off, and spent the rest of the day huddled by a nice warm heater.

Sometimes stories don't end so happily and promises are broken. When my wife, Celine, was a little girl in the Philippines, her mother sent her on an errand one day. She gave Celine some money and asked her to buy meat at the marketplace.

On the way to the market, an older woman came up to Celine and asked why she was by herself. Celine explained about the meat-buying mission. The woman smiled and said she was good friends with Celine's mother. She said if Celine would give her the money, she would go and purchase superior meat at a lower price. She assured Celine her mother would be pleased to save money. Celine hesitated, uncertain about handing over her cash to a stranger.

Seeing this, the woman pulled out a beautiful comb. She gave it to Celine as assurance that she would return with the meat. Celine studied the comb. The item was just enough to tip the scales. Gingerly Celine forked over the money. The woman patted Celine reassuringly on the head and promised to be right back.

But the woman never came back. After waiting and waiting, Celine finally realized the woman had lied. The comb became a sad reminder of a promise broken. Celine returned home that afternoon in tears. She received a scolding she remembers to this day.

Jesus Christ walked the earth for 33 years. He was born, He lived, He died. But He rose from the dead and now sits at the right hand of His Father in heaven. But before He left, Jesus promised to leave something for us—a reminder that one day He will return in fulfillment of His promises. For Christians, this deposit provides great comfort. We live in a world of great suffering and pain. Time, wrinkles, and death will eventually catch up with all of us. When we go through tough times, when our 15 minutes of fame are up, when we realize the firm foundation on which we built our lives has really been thin ice and we suddenly find ourselves plunged into freezing waters, that is when we fully grasp the blessing of the "wool cap" Jesus left behind for us—the Holy Spirit!

As the years whip by, as youthful hopes and dreams melt away, as parents age and grow weak with illness no matter how much we pray they won't, as bad things continue to happen to good people, sometimes the only place to find peace—to be lifted out of freezing waters and go to a place where our souls can dry off as we curl up in front of a nice warm heater—is in the hope and comfort Jesus left behind in the person of the Holy Spirit.

He anointed us, set his seal of ownership on us, and put his Spirit in our hearts as a deposit, guaranteeing what is to come (2 Corinthians 1:21-22).

Consider This

What things of this world do you put your hope in? What things of God do you put your hope in? Which have been more reliable?

A Time to Bless
Our Times Are in God's Hands

No one can confidently say that
he will still be living tomorrow.

EURIPIDES

Jack was our first Welsh corgi. He was beautiful, smart, and full of life. He loved my husband, Steve, so much that every time Steve stretched out on the living room floor to rest, Jack would lie right next to him. He also followed Steve around the house. He was a puppy and still learning the ways of our home. Through it all, he was a sweet blessing—and we adored him.

One afternoon when I was at my mom's, Steve came home for lunch and decided to lie down on the floor with Jack to take a quick nap. When he left for work again, Jack seemed to be sleeping soundly so Steve quietly slipped out the front door. He got into his pickup, put it into reverse, and started to back down the driveway. Suddenly he felt a thud. Jumping out of the truck, Steve ran behind it and found Jack, now lifeless, lying beside the rear tire. Without Steve being aware of it, Jack had run out the door behind him, following his master.

After Steve called to tell me, I raced home. We both wept over our puppy's body. We knew how much we would miss this little guy. We were such a good match…but I guess it was only to be for a season. We had Jack just four months, and the time was much too short.

We've had other dogs much longer. McPherson, Huxley, and Max passed away because they were old and their bodies were worn out. They were great pals and special members of our family. The last time Steve took Max to the vet, the doctor looked at the dog, did a few tests, and quietly observed that Max had lived a good, long life but there wasn't much left of him anymore. We'd all said our goodbyes, but there were plenty of tears shed that evening… and in many evenings that followed.

Just as our dogs have blessed our lives for short and long times, so has it been with the human ones we've loved. Our baby twins, born in 1976, lived less than a day. We were blessed by Steven's sweet smile and by the peaceful look on his face after his spirit had gone to heaven. Erin's fight to live inspired those who could see her tiny hands waving in her baby warmer. I was blessed by the incredible time I had with her in her last hours and as I felt her presence leave her body to go to her heavenly Father.

Like Max, my mom lived a long and fulfilled life. She was a blessing to everyone who knew her. She was old and done living when she passed away just before her ninety-second birthday. I know she's in heaven and I'm glad, but I miss her terribly too.

Mom and I had some very special times in her last years. They were so sweet and precious to my heart. When Mom was 89, she fell. Because she broke some ribs, she came to stay with Steve and me for several weeks. During that time I didn't go to work or follow my normal routine. She and I spent the time together. We laughed. We cried. Although it was difficult occasionally, we cherished the time.

Circumstances didn't allow me the closure I wanted with Mom when it came time for her to go to heaven. I'll always have a sad place in my heart about that. But when I think of that time we had together, I can hear her say, "Just let it go," and I have peace.

Yesterday I went to the cemetery where Mom's body is. Her headstone isn't made yet, but the marker is there with her name on it. Dad's stone is next to hers. He passed away nearly 35 years ago. I started crying as I thought about how much I missed them. Then a warm, pure peace came over me as I thought how happy they must be together again. I felt as though they were telling me how joyful they are. The experience didn't stop there. I felt like generations of grandpas and grandmas were telling me that God is with me.

And not only did I feel the presence of old people, but the gentle, dear presence of our baby twins filled my heart. I got into my car and drove over to their little gravesite. They share a beautiful headstone that's nice to look at, but I know they are with Jesus.

Steven and Erin were with us for a short time of blessings. Our dog Jack was with us a few months. Dad was in my life until I was twenty-one. Mom, Max, Huxley, and McPherson were long-lifers. Each was a blessing during the time God allowed them to live on earth.

Solomon wrote, "There is a time for everything, and a season for every activity under heaven: a time to be born and a time to die" (Ecclesiastes 3:1-2). Only God knows what that time is for me, and I'm grateful I don't need to worry about it. My prayer is simply that I will be a blessing to the people and animals God puts in my life during whatever time He gives me here on earth.

All the days ordained for me were written in your book before one of them came to be (Psalm 139:16).

Consider This

If you knew you were going to die tomorrow, what would you do that you aren't doing now? Is there anything you'd do differently? Would any behaviors and attitudes change? Why not consider living with this mindset all the time if it will help you serve God more fully and bless others more?

Boning Up I
Doggie Body Language

1. Can you make fearful dogs less so by adjusting your body position? If yes, how do you do it?

2. Does the way your dog wags its tail "tell a tale" about how it's feeling?

3. Why might smiling at a strange dog cause the dog to become aggressive?

4. What common thing do young children do that might give a dog the wrong message?

5. How does a dog signal that it wants to play?

Part 2

Paws for Training

Sit, Stay, Grow

SENATOR & NELLIE

For Love of the Master

Obedience Pleases God

Wicked men obey from fear;
good men, from love.

Aristotle

Nellie and Senator belong to my dear friends Glen and Susie. Nellie is a beautiful black Labrador that loves to play and perform for her loved ones. Senator is a handsome basset hound that likes to sit and watch.

One evening when I was visiting, Susie got out the doggie treats. She called Nellie and Senator. When Nellie saw the treats, she started wiggling all over. Susie told her to sit. She sat. Then she did more tricks: rolling over, playing dead, giving Susie her paw to shake, and performing a few more wonders…all without being told. She knew her performance would earn doggie treats, and she was out to get them.

Susie praised Nellie, hugged her, and gave the dog her well-earned reward. Susie was proud of Nellie, and I could see Nellie knew she'd done well and felt good that she'd delighted her master.

Senator, on the other hand, did nothing. He sat there as if he didn't care at all about pleasing his humans. We all laughed as we noted the "dopey" look on his face when he was asked to do something. Senator is smart and will obey in "real life" matters, but he refuses to do tricks when he's asked to entertain. Senator got a few treats too because Glen and Susie love him, but he didn't feel their pleasure the same way Nellie did. His disobedience caused him to miss out.

Humans also miss out when we fail to obey. My husband started playing trumpet in fourth grade. His parents told him to practice every day. Steve didn't want to, but he was obedient nonetheless. In time he was rewarded. He sat first chair trumpet in junior high and high school band and orchestra. He made honor band—comprised of the top musicians from area high schools—and sat first chair trumpet there also. His obedience enriched his young life...and even helped him meet his wife! (We met at a Youth for Christ state talent contest.)

Steve still plays trumpet. He's in our church's praise band and performs every Sunday. Many people are blessed through his music. Choosing to obey his earthly parents pleased them and eventually many others. Music provides a way for Steve to please his heavenly Father too.

As for me, I was more like Senator when it came to playing instruments. My parents provided piano lessons, but I didn't practice like I was told. Today I play very little. I only sit and listen. I missed the reward of obedience.

The Bible tells us that our obeying God pleases Him. It also says obedience to Him has rewards. We see this in the life of Hezekiah, king of Judah. In 2 Chronicles 31:20-21 we read, "This is what Hezekiah did throughout Judah, doing what was good and right and faithful before the LORD his God. In everything that he undertook in the service of God's temple and in obedience to the law and the commands, he sought his God and worked whole-heartedly. And so he prospered."

Jesus told His disciples, as recorded in John 14:15, "If you love me, you will obey what I command." They were not rewarded with material wealth, but they gained enormous spiritual blessings. And their obedience will be further rewarded in eternity by their heavenly Father, who is well pleased with them.

I love the Lord and want to please Him so He delights in me. I want to start every day by praying, "Lord, help me obey You!" I want to experience His pleasure and rewards here on earth and in His eternal kingdom! How about you?

If you obey my commands, you will remain in my love, just as I have obeyed my Father's commands and remain in his love (John 15:10).

Consider This

In what aspects of your life are you struggling to obey the Lord? What blessings are you missing as a result? What can you do to change this situation?

In what ways have you been obedient to God? What rewards did you receive? How did you know He was pleased?

The Load Not Taken
God's Burdens Bring Blessings

God gave burdens, also shoulders.

YIDDISH PROVERB

You're the dog lady, aren't you?"

A neighbor I barely knew had stopped me on my daily walk in my neighborhood. She said she needed advice, and soon I was standing in the middle of her kitchen meeting Lucy, her new red poodle puppy. Just a week after getting the dog, Sharon and her husband, Alvin, learned Lucy was deaf. They'd grown attached to the pup, but Sharon was afraid to keep her. Could she handle the care and training of a dog who couldn't hear? Or was this burden heavier than she could bear? And if it was too much, how could she make sure Lucy found a new home where she would get the love and attention she deserved?

I could see how torn Sharon felt. I could also see that Lucy was a wonderful dog. I had no direct experience with Sharon's dilemma, but I did have a "go to" person. My friend Cindy is deeply involved in animal rescue. I said I'd phone her and see if she could be of any help.

Cindy's words were reassuring. Unbeknownst to me, one of Cindy's dogs was also deaf. My friend hadn't found it all that difficult to deal with either. There were trainers who knew how to work with hearing-impaired animals. Cindy said she would speak with Sharon and offer her some resources and insights. And if Sharon still felt it best to give Lucy up, Cindy had a friend with experience finding homes for special-needs dogs.

I shared this input with Sharon and gave her Cindy's number.

Days passed and I forgot about Sharon's situation. Then I bumped into her again, and she told me Lucy was going to stay with them.

Sharon and Alvin have had some challenges raising Lucy. Their biggest issue is safety. If Lucy were to escape from their house or yard by accident, she wouldn't hear them calling her. She also wouldn't hear sounds of danger, such as the engine of an oncoming car. They also don't allow Lucy off leash unless she's in a very safe place.

Training and disciplining Lucy has also been tricky. They've taught her hand signals, but those only work when she can see them. If Lucy's in another room, they can't just call her. They have to get up and go get her. They also can't use voice inflections to reveal praise or disapproval. They've had to come up with innovative ways to get their messages across.

Even so, Sharon and Alvin have no regrets about keeping Lucy. They love her to bits. Sharon says Lucy has an unusually sweet temperament. She's so good with everyone, including children, that Sharon has even thought about looking into doing hospital visitations with the dog. The extra burdens Lucy's masters have shouldered are more than outweighed by the countless ways she was blessed their lives.

My friend Hana also shouldered a burden that brought blessing. Like Sharon, she wasn't sure she could handle it at first. She
nearly fled from the load many times...until she finally felt led of
God to take on the challenge of being my mother's nurse.

I met Hana when Mom was desperately ill and in the hospital.
A potent skin infection had spread to her blood. Mom wanted
caregivers with her every second in addition to the hospital staff,
so I called a nursing service. Hana was the first person they sent.

Mom took to Hana instantly, but it wasn't mutual. My tiny
mother was flat on her back, deathly sick, but she still commanded
the room. Add to her strong personality the fear of dying, disori-
entation from lack of sleep, and the heavy-duty drugs she was on,
and Mom ran her help ragged.

Hana told me later that every time she finished a shift caring
for Mom, she vowed she wouldn't return. But every time something made her relent, and she came back. Meanwhile, Mom had
bonded with Hana and asked her to quit the agency and work
full-time for her.

Hana and I share a deep faith in God. We both believe the
burden of Mom's care was guided by His hand. Recently Hana
shared what had finally convinced her to take the job. Mom told
Hana that though she had a lot of people around her, deep inside
she was a very lonely woman. She felt a deep connection with
Hana and wanted her companionship.

Sharon's dog-shaped burden proved relatively light. Hana's was
crushingly heavy at times. Mom had other nurses who worked
hard and loved her dearly...and she loved them. But she counted
on Hana most, and when she felt sickest or most frightened, she
wanted Hana with her. When Mom's health suffered major set-
backs, Hana worked many hours. Mom would get scared about
dying so she'd be afraid to sleep. Because she stayed up all night,

she wanted to talk (nonstop!) and didn't want to be left alone for even a minute. It was exhausting for Hana. But by leaning on God, she was able to let Mom lean on her. She even managed to steer the conversation to how faith in God could ease Mom's fear of death. And when Mom was about to walk through the door of this world to what lies beyond, Hana joined me in a bedside vigil until Mom slipped away.

After Mom's death I took Hana out to dinner. She was taking time off to recuperate. Glad as she was to finally rest, she told me, "I'm going to miss that lady."

Hana said Mom was a role model who taught her a lot. She admired Mom's strength, positive outlook, hard work ethic, and her belief in herself. She was inspired by how Mom always reached out to help others. Working for her had been a burden, but it had been a blessing too.

Sharon and Hana faced burdens they weren't sure they were up for. I believe this happens to all of us. The consummate illustration of this is Jesus. He faced dying on a wooden cross for the sins of the world. In the Garden of Gethsemane, He prayed, "Father, if you are willing, take this cup from me; yet not my will, but yours be done" (Luke 22:42).

Jesus chose to follow God's plan. He bore the burden of our sins and became the instrument of our salvation. Paul tells us, "Therefore God exalted him to the highest place and gave him the name that is above every name, that at the name of Jesus every knee should bow, in heaven and on earth and under the earth, and every tongue confess that Jesus Christ is Lord, to the glory of God the Father" (Philippians 2:9-11).

Like Jesus, we have things God has appointed us to do. We choose how we will respond to His call. If we take the burden on and rely on God, He will help us carry it and bless our obedience.

Anyone who does not take his cross and follow me is not worthy of me. Whoever finds his life will lose it, and whoever loses his life for my sake will find it (Matthew 10:38-39).

Consider This

Has God asked you to take on a burden you didn't want? Did you respond in obedience? If so, how did God help you? What blessings did you experience?

The Walk That Got Away
Seize Your Opportunities

A wise man will make more
opportunities than he finds.

Francis Bacon

When I was single and went on vacation, my roommate, Carl, would take care of my dog, Gracie. Carl loved my kooky and adorable mutt with her low-slung corgi body and German shepherd head. Carl and I have many fond memories of Gracie, who has since passed away, but there is one situation that occasionally haunts my friend.

Sometimes after a long day at work, Carl would come home, slouch on the couch with soda and pizza within easy reach on the coffee table, and watch a sit-com or baseball game on TV. Only a major earthquake or a desperate need to use the bathroom could dislodge Carl from his little slice of bachelor heaven on earth.

Then he'd hear a sound. He'd tear his gaze away from the TV and look around to see Gracie staring at him from across the room. She would poke at the door, dog sign language for "Get off your behind and take me for a walk!" This was serious business for

Gracie. Along with napping and eating, taking her nightly walk was the biggest deal of her daily existence. And while Carl usually accommodated her requests, sometimes the gravitational pull of the couch was too much to overcome.

Years later, when Carl came to visit, he'd look at our front door and remember Gracie staring at him with her soulful brown eyes, her tail wagging with enough velocity to fly a small plane as she patiently waited for Carl to grab the leash. But after a while, she would give up and settle down on the floor, a morose groan revealing her sorrow. He also recalled Gracie's dying days, when her health had deteriorated and she could barely stand. And then he'd remember and wonder, "Geez, would it have killed me to take her for extra walks on those lazy afternoons?"

I also have missed opportunities that haunt me. Many years ago my mother asked me to accompany her to Egypt to see the pyramids. Because I was in a new relationship, I decided to stay home. Unfortunately the romantic relationship ended, and as the years flew by my hopes of visiting the pyramids dissolved into the regret of a missed opportunity. And I hadn't just missed the chance to get up close to one of the Seven Wonders of the World. I had also missed spending irreplaceable time with my mother. I still visit with my mom, but she has a lot of trouble walking these days. It's difficult for her to climb into a car, let alone navigate a huge pyramid.

Some of the opportunities we miss are more subtle. This year my wife and I made a commitment to read through Oswald Chambers' classic devotional *My Utmost for His Highest*. We know it's good for us as a daily reminder that being rightly related to God must be our primary concern. We feel this book speaks truth to us and helps draw us closer to Christ and to each other. That said, it's amazing how often we put off our reading until the last waking moments of the day, when we're both so tired that all we want to do is lie down and dissolve into the mattress. On those nights, usually right before we're about to fall asleep, we hear a "scratching on our souls" and remember we haven't read our Oswald yet. We realize how many opportunities we had to read the devotional during the day but chose other things—watching TV, reading a magazine or newspaper, making phone calls, checking email for the fifth time in the same hour. We acknowledge how spending daily devotional time together enriches our lives and our marriage and improves how we raise our son and treat our neighbors. Then, like Carl on the couch, we still choose to ignore the pawing on the door of our hearts—the still small voice of God—and wind up giving in to the inertia of sleep. The next day there's a twinge of regret for not having spent time with God in a yesterday that will never come back.

Carl shared many happy times with Gracie. I still visit my parents. Celine and I continue to read Oswald. And God says He will never leave us or forsake us—even if we don't always spend time with Him when we can and should. Let's remember to take advantage of the many opportunities to create special memories and realize well-timed insights that beckon only once.

Much as we regret the "earthly" opportunities that have slipped away, there is a heavenly one that would be infinitely worse to miss. Jesus said, "For God so loved the world that he gave his one and only Son, that whoever believes in him shall not perish but have eternal life" (John 3:16). God offers us the incredible choice to have our sins forgiven and spend eternity in His love and presence. He gives us opportunities to share this tremendous blessing with others. Surely the greatest regret of all—the one to be avoided at all costs—is to spend forever regretting eternal separation from God. In light of that, let's seize every moment we can to know Him more and share His love and plan with others.

And being in torments in Hades, he lifted up his eyes and saw Abraham afar off, and Lazarus in his bosom. Then he cried and said, "Father Abraham, have mercy on me, and send Lazarus that he may dip the tip of his finger in water and cool my tongue; for I am tormented in this flame."

But Abraham said, "Son, remember that in your lifetime you received your good things, and likewise Lazarus evil things; but now he is comforted and you are tormented. And besides all this, between us and you there is a great gulf fixed, so that those who want to pass from here to you cannot, nor can those from there pass to us" (Luke 16:23-26 NKJV).

Consider This

What are the greatest regrets of your life? Can any of them be undone? Being eternally separated from God is the greatest sorrow of all. Are there loved ones you can reach out to with the good news of Jesus before it's too late?

Squitchey on Patrol
Look to God for Protection

*Safety does not depend on our conception of
the absence of danger.
Safety is found in God's presence,
in the center of His perfect will.*

T.J. Bach

Our community depends on our sheriff, deputies, and police to protect us from criminals. We count on firefighters to save us from fire. But our family has an extra advantage when it comes to being guarded. Only we have "The Squitchmeister"!

Squitchey has a "superdog" passion to keep her family safe... but her definition of danger doesn't always match ours. This seven-pound mass of dog hair and determination darts out the doggie door on red alert at the sound of helicopters, motorcycles, lawn-mowers, and tractors. She races around the yard barking furiously to frighten the enemies away.

Squitchey also chases birds. If there's more than one in the yard, she tears after them, even jumping into trees to try to catch them. She hasn't gotten any yet, but we've had to pull pine tree needles and twigs from her fur many times.

Part of Squitchey's strategy to scare off intruders, be they animal or mechanical, is to run in tight circles and woof until they leave. Eventually they all do, and she marches back inside a hero, announcing that she has once again saved us from harm. She doesn't know that we weren't in harm's way. She's doing her duty—protecting her family from danger the best she can. And we love her for it!

Like Squitchey, my husband is determined to protect our family. And sometimes Steve overreacts too. Years ago our family went to Israel. We were walking where Jesus walked, seeing Bible stories come alive as we stood where He stood. At one point a vendor was trying to aggressively sell something to our children and me. This man's actions made Steve uncomfortable, so he physically put himself between the fellow and our family. He guided us back on the tour bus and asked the man to leave us alone. Looking back, Steve thinks we probably weren't in any real danger. There was most likely a cultural misunderstanding. The hard-working vendor was probably trying a little too hard to make money from the American tourists and meant no harm. At the time, though, Steve felt the need to step in and protect his beloved family from the potential threat.

Dogs and humans don't always know true threats from false. They don't always spot real danger. And they can't always be present with their loved ones to keep them safe from harm. But our all-knowing, all-powerful, all-loving God can!

When our children were little, Steve and I prayed for them every day before they went to school. When they went to camp or anywhere away from us, we prayed for God's protection around them. We continue to lift them up now that they are grown and live on their own. And we hear stories of how God guards them and keeps them safe.

Our daughter, Karen, and her friend Alyssa spent a few months studying abroad when they were in college. Early one morning they were in Scotland near a bus station. A man walked up to them and asked if they were looking for a hostel to stay in. They said they were. He told them about one and offered to take them there in his car. They politely refused. He insisted. No one else was around. The young adults felt uneasy and knew they needed to get away from the situation, so they did. They feel God protected them from possible harm.

Squitchey protects us in the best way she can because she loves us. Steve and I knew the best ways to safeguard our children were to bring them before God and teach them to put on the full armor of God (Ephesians 6). We've done this, and it's worked well for them. We are grateful that our heavenly Father is "an ever-present help in trouble" who is always and forever watching over them... and us.

God is our refuge and strength, an ever-present help in trouble... The LORD Almighty is with us; the God of Jacob is our fortress (Psalm 46:1,7).

Consider This

What is the greatest danger you've ever faced? To whom or to what did you look for help? What was the result? Has God kept you from danger? How?

Lessons from an Alpha

Submit to the Lord

If God asks that you bend,
bend and do not complain.
He is making you more flexible,
and for this be thankful.

Meriel Stelliger

Pastor John Scoggins has a wonderful relationship with his black Lab named Buq. It began when Buq was born. John was walking Buq's mother, Lucy, when the dog stopped. John thought she was going to relieve herself, but instead she was giving birth! When John realized what was happening, he dropped her leash, hurried up to her, and caught Lucy's first and only pup in his hands.

John named his new little guy Buq'A Rue. He wanted the spelling to be special. John says Buq is the most exuberant dog he's ever known. Fortunately Buq understands that John is the alpha or "top dog" in his world, and it's a good thing because sometimes Buq's exuberance has gotten him into trouble.

One day John and his wife, Sharon, came home from doing errands and only Lucy showed up to greet them. They were concerned because usually both dogs ran to meet them. They looked around the backyard. They found Buq with his head stuck in an oval watering can. He had wedged the can on his head and couldn't get it off. If the spout of the watering can had gone into the dirt, he would have suffocated. As it was, Buq was plenty scared. John calmed him down and removed the can. Now, Buq doesn't like his head being handled in any way. But when John is playing with him and holds his head, Buq submits. He knows John is in control.

John trains his dogs with love and positive reinforcement. All he needs to do is point at Buq and the dog will stop what he is doing and go where John tells him to. It doesn't work quite the same when John's wife is in charge. When Sharon takes Buq and Lucy for a walk, people comment that it looks as though the dogs are taking her because her arms are pulled straight and the leashes are taut. But as soon as John takes over and gives the leashes a little tug, the dogs come to attention and walk obediently by his side. Buq and Lucy know John is the alpha among them, and they act accordingly.

Training his dogs has helped John understand the love and concern God has when He trains us. God wants us to obey Him for our own good. But we don't always respond that way, and then He must discipline us because He loves us.

John recalls a time in his life when God asserted Himself as John's "Alpha." John was in his third semester at Dallas Theological Seminary. He'd grown up in a dysfunctional home and didn't come to know Christ as his Savior until late in his junior year at a Christian university. After that, for reasons that are unclear to him, he decided to pursue a seminary education. He and his young wife moved to Dallas, but he was hardly a viable candidate for the pastoral ministry at that point. He was very rough around the edges. He was going through cart-before-the-horse doubts about his calling. Why was he here? How did he get here? What was he doing?

Meanwhile, he was also working part-time as a carpenter to support his wife and infant daughter. Early in his third semester, he fell from a building he was working on and sustained a serious injury. Times were already tough financially, and now it got much worse. He was collecting a whopping $49 a week in workman's compensation. Bills were adding up. He was unable to make tuition payments, and his family was scraping by with barely enough groceries. By the time he was ready to go back to work, he was forced to drop out of school to catch up financially. He thought he would return to school the next fall. He wasn't able to then…or for a long time after. No matter how hard he tried, God blocked his reentry into seminary for the next two-and-a-half years. It hurt a lot, but God had a reason for the pain. He was smoothing out rough spots in John's character while reaffirming his call to ministry.

In that process, John came to realize that what mattered most was not getting back into school. Instead, it was submitting to God's direction and discipline in his life. As his sensitivity to God's leading increased and his heart attitude changed, the door opened for him to continue his education.

Buq showed John that it's important to know where the "watering cans" of life are and what they can do. God's Word warns us about these, and John points them out in his sermons to help his congregation. But there are still times when we get our heads stuck in something! Our loving Master calms us down and frees us.

John's dogs show by their actions that their master is their "alpha." God is John's Alpha, so God has authority over him. If John trots obediently at the side of his Master, God is pleased and makes John's path straight.

Our fathers disciplined us for a little while as they thought best; but God disciplines us for our good, that we may share in his holiness. No discipline seems pleasant at the time, but painful. Later on, however, it produces a harvest of righteousness and peace for those who have been trained by it (Hebrews 12:10-11).

Consider This

Have you gotten your head stuck in a "watering can"? Why did you stick your head in it? How were you endangered? How did God get your head out? How has God been training you in your walk with Him? What have you learned that you can share with others?

Great Expectations
Be Persistent in Prayer

'Tis expectation makes a blessing dear;
Heaven were not Heaven, if we knew what it were.

Sir John Suckling

This morning our dog Stuart had an appointment at the vet's office. It was time to do some routine blood work to make sure his epilepsy medication wasn't causing any problems. My husband decided to put Stuart's harness on early so he'd be ready to go when it came time. Steve got the harness and called Stuart. Stuart sat quietly while Steve wrapped the straps around his body and made it comfortable for him. Then Stuart jumped up and ran to the front door. He was expecting his master to take him for a walk right away. That's what the harness usually meant.

Steve is a busy farmer, and he really needed to get to work. But he didn't want to disappoint his dog either. He and Stuart happily took a short walk down the road and back. Stuart's eager expectation was rewarded.

I know people who live with the philosophy that if you don't expect anything, you won't be disappointed. Their expectations are confined by the dread of the bad things they fear might happen. Isn't that sad? Some people, like my daughter, live with excited anticipation of the good things that may come to pass.

A while after graduating from college, Karen and her friend Alyssa decided they really wanted to work at Disneyland. They'd spent a lot of enjoyable time and had many fun experiences there when they were in college and living close to Anaheim. They both applied and then prayed to God with eager anticipation. They asked that He would allow this for them. Both of them were hired.

Karen is a tour guide and takes great pride in how she shares information. She uses her vivid imagination to choose words and examples that spice up her presentations. She shares Walt Disney's stories in a way that makes him come alive for the tourists. But Karen was terrified in the beginning. She had five days to memorize 35 pages of information before her first tour. She was to guide 13 paying guests for three hours. Her expectations were dread oriented. She told me later that she was so nervous she thought she'd have a heart attack. But then she gave the situation to the Lord. She prayed expectantly, knowing He loved her and had put her there. God answered—and the tour went smoothly.

Karen's expectations were met rather quickly. Sometimes it takes a lot longer, and we can grow weary in waiting for God to act. Several years ago our community experienced a serious drought. Many of the farmers in the area got together once a week to pray for rain. The drought was of deep concern because the crops were dying. The farmers pleaded desperately with God. Some of them doubted God would act and got discouraged. Others waited with hopeful anticipation for rain to fall. Eventually it did. The fields were saved, and the farmers came together again to thank their Creator for answering their prayers. In a way they were just like

Stuart—walking happily with their Master, pleased that their expectations had been rewarded.

Stuart, Karen, and most of the farmers had good reasons to count on the fulfillment of their expectations. Stuart assumed he'd get his walk because his master loves him. Karen knew her heavenly Master loves her and will do what's best for her. She prayed with eager anticipation of being hired at Disneyland because she trusted if it didn't work out, God had something better planned. And most of the farmers realized that though they didn't control the rain, God did—and He would take care of them.

Life has uncertainties for all of us. God gives us all the choice to face the future with eager anticipation or dread. Though we won't always get what we ask for or think we have to have, we can pray with great expectations because we can trust God's wisdom over our own and rest in His love and provision.

I have carried you since you were born; I have taken care of you from your birth. Even when you are old, I will be the same. Even when your hair has turned gray, I will take care of you. I made you and will take care of you. I will carry you and save you (Isaiah 46:3-4 NCV).

Consider This

What "great expectations" of yours has God said yes to? What are you expectantly praying for right now?

Whose Kibble Is It, Anyway?
All We Have Belongs to God

*One of the greatest missing teachings in the
American church today is the reminder to
men and women that nothing we have belongs to us.*

GORDON MACDONALD

My dogs understand perfectly well that I am the source of their kibble, and that I dispense it in the morning. They have the routine down perfectly. Race out the back door to do their business and charge back in for feeding time. Sit at the screen door or leap at it to hurry things along. Once inside, they stampede to the feeding station and bury their heads in the bowls that are being lowered for them. Only if absolutely necessary will they sit and stay during a moment of tortured obedience training before being released to inhale their breakfast.

Biscuit, Morgan, and Becca understand that their kibble comes from me, their master. But do they understand it still belongs to me once it hits their bowls? I doubt it. I believe they think it becomes theirs. Morgan's actions support this conclusion. He often takes the longest to eat. If one of the other dogs edges toward his bowl to steal a bite, he is apt to growl a warning.

This sense of doggie proprietorship extends to treats as well. Recently I rewarded the dogs with bone-shaped breath-freshening yummies. They each grabbed their goody, trotted off to a separate spot on the floor, and flopped down to demolish their prize. Because I'm their master, it's not likely they would have bitten me if I'd decided to take back their bones. But I doubt the thought I might steal their treats even entered their brains. These treats were theirs alone to eat, and that's all they concentrated on.

As their master, I can't blame them for such an approach. They aren't wired for complex thinking, and they aren't made in my image. But we humans have been created in the image of our heavenly Father. And He desires that we have a very different attitude toward the "kibble" He provides. He desires we recognize that absolutely everything we are and have comes from Him, is still His, and will always be His.

God brought this principle home to me in a new and unexpected fashion. Some months ago my mom passed away, leaving me coexecutor and primary beneficiary of her estate. She'd been deeply and passionately involved in the work of a couple of nonprofit organizations. She expressed a wish in her will that a small family foundation be dissolved and its assets be divided between them. While it seemed likely the foundation's board would be willing to honor Mom's wishes, we discovered that some corporate "housekeeping" hadn't been done. It would take time to sort out the legalities and bring everything up-to-date so the money could be disbursed.

Meanwhile, one of the designated charities started to feel a serious financial pinch. Mom had provided a significant portion of their annual budget. With her gone and the foundation gift delayed, they saw a serious shortfall looming. I was seeking God's guidance relative to my own giving, and I felt His call to honor

Mom in the use of what she'd left to me. But my passions were different than hers, and I hadn't planned to step into her shoes with her nonprofit interests. Now I was feeling major guilt. Mom would have written a check for the organization were she alive. And my inheritance came from her. It was her money...or at least used to be her money. Should I pay what she would have?

I wrestled with my thoughts and sought the Lord. God spoke to my heart and straightened out my thinking: "Your inheritance was from your mom, but it wasn't hers. It was Mine. It will always be Mine. And it's Mine now."

I felt a weight lift off my shoulders. This insight from God freed me to hear His guidance more clearly. As I kept praying and seeking godly human counsel, another choice emerged that caused me to feel great peace and joy. I suggested the organization launch a special fund-raising campaign. As an incentive to their donors, if they hit certain monetary goals, I'd provide specific additional sums.

They were successful and, in the process, widened their donor base. Mom had always wanted them to do that. The organization was thrilled, and I let them know the role my prayers and my friends' prayers had played in the situation. I told them God was the source of the financial blessing. God also graciously allowed our family foundation's legalities to get sorted out so disbursements could take place.

I'm all too human. Just because I get it right once in a while doesn't mean I always will. Even as I recognize God's ownership of one area of my life, I might seek to hold back in another. For instance, I might lay my "time" bank account at His feet, only to snatch it back, trot off to my favorite private corner, and gnaw a whole day away as if it belonged just to me.

Many centuries ago God spoke to the Israelites through Moses:

"Now if you obey me fully and keep my covenant, then out of all nations you will be my treasured possession. Although the whole earth is mine, you will be for me a kingdom of priests and a holy nation" (Exodus 19:5-6).

All we are and have is God's, whether we acknowledge it or not. But if we do, we'll draw closer to Him. As we seek His guidance to use what He entrusts us with for His glory, we will know His pleasure and reap eternal fruit for His kingdom.

If I were hungry I would not tell you, for the world is mine, and all that is in it (Psalm 50:12).

Consider This

In what areas of your life (time, talents, possessions, money, relationships) do you find it most difficult to acknowledge God's ownership? Why do you think this is so? How might you yield these more completely to God? What difference do you think this will make?

Stolen Shoes
Know Why You Believe

*Those who pin their faith on other men's sleeves,
and walk in the way of the world,
have turned away from following after Christ.*

MATTHEW HENRY

Rocky was Great-Grandpa Fleishauer's first dog. He was a Queensland healer and lived outdoors on the farm. When his master was outside, Rocky stayed right beside him. They played fetch and walked the grounds together. He was a great pet and watchdog. Great-Grandpa loved him dearly...except for one thing. Rocky had a thing for shoes.

Our family still tells the story of the meter reader who came into the yard unaware of Rocky's shoe fetish. Rocky jumped on him, knocked him down, tore off both his shoes, and took them somewhere. By the time Great-Grandpa got outside, the utility man was sitting on the lawn, laughing in a relieved sort of way... probably because nothing worse had happened. It must have been a shock to suddenly have the firm foundation of his shoes (and feet) pulled out from under him. Rocky's master explained that this was his dog's strange way of protecting his family and playing with his friends. Rocky didn't hurt the man, and wouldn't have, but I'm guessing that meter reader was more careful in the future.

After Great-Grandpa died, Rocky went to live with my husband's father. It worked out well, except Rocky still had his "shoe thing" going. One time the water softener man walked into the yard before any human saw him. My husband's mom heard a yell and ran out to see what had happened. The guy told her she was too late—the dog had gotten one of his shoes. She apologized, retrieved it, and gave it back. After that he never failed to announce his arrival by whistling loudly as he headed for the backyard. He and Rocky got to be friends, but that didn't mean his shoes were safe!

Rocky's antics made me realize how important our shoes are to us. This is true not just physically, but spiritually also. When I was teaching at a private Christian school, my class once planned a chapel time with the theme "Putting on Your Spiritual Shoes." As we worked on this program we talked a lot about the armor of God. Ephesians 6:14-15 says, "Stand firm then, with the belt of truth buckled around your waist, with the breastplate of righteousness in place, and with your feet fitted with the readiness that comes from the gospel of peace."

Bible scholars draw different conclusions about what the footwear is in this verse. I think we can safely say that if we know what and why we believe, and realize we have peace with God because Jesus died for us, it will help us stand firm in our faith and walk according to God's ways. As my students studied, rehearsed, talked, and prayed, they learned how important it is to be ready with the armor of God. One boy told me about a problem he'd had with another boy on the playground. This other boy wanted him to disobey the rules...in essence taking off his spiritual shoes and running barefoot in the world. But my student said he put on the armor of God, fit his feet with readiness, and walked away from trouble!

Unlike the men who walked into Rocky's yard unprepared for trouble, my student was ready to resist a spiritual attack. He knew what and why he believed, and he stood strong. If we stay grounded in Jesus and know God's Word, we are wearing our spiritual shoes. We'll have victory in Him!

Be strong in the Lord and in his mighty power. Put on the full armor of God so that you can take your stand against the devil's schemes (Ephesians 6:10-11).

Consider This

When was the last time someone tried to pull your spiritual shoes off? How did you respond? What can you do to be better prepared next time? In what ways do you don your spiritual armor and keep it polished?

Sign Language
Watch for God's Miracles

*Miracles are a retelling in small letters of the very
same story which is written across the
whole world in letters too large for some of us to see.*

C.S. LEWIS

Shane, Mary's one-year-old chocolate Lab, woke her in the middle of the night by laying his head on the bed and licking her face. He whimpered insistently. Mary got up and checked him out. His front leg was swollen. By morning his abdomen had also become swollen and distended. The vet couldn't find a cause and sent him home with antibiotics and pain medicine. Shane got worse and was soon hospitalized. He rapidly declined over the next few days. The vet's only option was exploratory surgery. It was then that the cause of the problem surfaced. He had been bitten under his leg...by a rattlesnake.

It had been five days since the bite. The vet told Mary her dog wouldn't recover from the attack. Mary was devastated, as was her seven-year-old son, Stephen. For the next couple of days Mary and Stephen brought Shane his favorite foods, hoping to entice him to eat. But nothing worked. Shane's organs were shutting down, and his physical symptoms indicated he didn't have much longer to live.

Mary was heartbroken. With tears streaming down her cheeks, she held Shane's face up to hers and told him he had to get well. Stephen needed him…the entire family needed him! At that moment Mary saw what she describes as a glimmer of light pass through Shane's eyes. She held him and sobbed. Perhaps this was the prelude to his passing. But Shane did something unexpected. With all his strength and resolve, he lifted his head, reached over, and took a small bite of the baby food meat stick Mary had been holding for him. Mary blinked away the tears and knew in her heart this was a sign that God was going to intervene. As the doctors offered their well-meaning condolences, Mary took Shane home and confidently nursed him back to health. When she returned a month later with her healthy dog in tow, the vets were speechless. They said it was a miracle—and it was!

I've also received a sign from God. When my wife was about to give birth to our first (and only) child, instead of inviting me into the delivery room, a concerned nurse asked me to wait outside because there were "complications." As I sat alone mulling this worrisome news, my heart sank. What if something was terribly wrong? I thought of my cousin, whose mother had died giving birth. What if I lost Celine? Or what if Celine lost the baby, and we were to be childless?

I cried out to God, "Please keep Celine well and bring our child safely into this world." As I bowed my head, something prompted me to reach into my shirt pocket. I pulled out a couple of business cards with scriptures I'd written on the back so I could memorize them. I'd forgotten I'd stuck them in this pocket. As I looked at a verse I'd scribbled down a few days ago, it was as if I was looking at a prophecy. It was Malachi 4:2: "For you who revere my name, the sun of righteousness will rise with healing in its wings. And you will go out and leap like calves released from the stall."

At that moment I knew Celine and my *son* were going to be all right. I emphasize "son" because we'd chosen not to find out if we were going to have a girl or a boy. We wanted to be surprised on the day of birth. So when the verse said the "sun" shall rise with healing in its wings, I took that as a creative double-meaning pun from God—a sign to assure me that we would have a healthy son. And the part about leaping like a calf released from a stall? I took this to mean that this would be a relatively quick and easy birth, and our son would be a very active guy. Instantly God's peace that transcends all understanding came over me (Philippians 4:7). I knew God had answered my prayers. In a few moments, the nurse came out and said the complications had uncomplicated themselves. She invited me back in to watch the birth of my child—a seven-pound eleven-ounce "son of righteousness." And seven years later I can attest that he has the energy of a little calf or a small bull or maybe both.

When Mary's dog, Shane, was sick and dying from his rattlesnake bite, the doctors relied on modern, scientific, medical signs to make their "dog is hopeless" prognosis. When Celine was in the hospital about to give birth, the doctors relied on modern, scientific, medical signs to warn me there were complications with our baby's delivery. But just as doctors and scientists get signs from their instruments and machines, those who have "eyes to see and ears to hear" get signs from God. These signs are not discerned by our biological eyes, but by the eyes of our hearts. We can choose to see them…or not. When a heart "sees" a dying dog eat a small snack and knows the dog will live, when a heart "reads" a prophetic verse pulled from a shirt pocket and knows his wife will give birth to a healthy son—we are seeing and believing signs by faith. When this happens, when our hearts see God's blessing before it materializes, we are viewing the reality to come as being real now, living out the Hebrews 11:1 definition of faith: "Faith is being sure of what we hope for and certain of what we do not see."

There are also many Bible stories about God giving signs to people to encourage them. One of the most amazing concerns Hezekiah, an ancient king of Judah. He was ill, and Isaiah, God's prophet, told him he would soon die. And if that weren't bad enough, Judah was about to be besieged by Sennacherib, the fearsome king of Assyria, who sent his chief-of-staff to tell Hezekiah how much the Jews would suffer. Sennacherib's man warned Hezekiah, "They will be so hungry and thirsty that they will eat their own dung and drink their own urine" (2 Kings 18:27 NLT). Then he issued an ultimatum to Hezekiah and his people: Surrender now—or die! He summed up his master's threat in 2 Kings 18:35 NLT: "What god of any nation has ever been able to save its people from my power? So what makes you think that the LORD can rescue Jerusalem from me?"

Talk about problems! But Hezekiah did what we all can do today. He prayed! He talked to the same God Mary did when begging for the life of her rattlesnake-bitten dog and to the same God I pleaded with for mercy on my wife and unborn child. As Hezekiah wept bitterly, Isaiah delivered good news—that the Lord would add 15 years to Hezekiah's life and deliver his city from the king of Assyria. Then God gave Hezekiah one doozy of a sign. We find out what it was in Isaiah 38:7-8 MSG: "'And this is your confirming sign, confirming that I, GOD, will do exactly what I have promised. Watch for this: As the sun goes down and the shadow lengthens on the sundial of Ahaz, I'm going to reverse the shadow ten notches on the dial.' And that's what happened: The declining sun's shadow reversed ten notches on the dial."

Did you get that? The same God who got a dying dog to nibble a snack and who provided an anxious father-to-be with an uplifting scripture *moved the sun backward* as a sign of encouragement to one of His children. And that same God still gives His children signs and does miracles today. So as you pray and look to the Lord for help—be encouraged. Your heavenly Father loves you!

Therefore the Lord himself will give you a sign (Isaiah 7:14).

Consider This

Did God give you a sign to encourage you in a specific situation? What blessing did it promise that hadn't happened yet? How was it fulfilled?

Timex Dog
Keep on Ticking for the Master

Success is not final, failure is not fatal:
It is the courage to continue that counts.

Sir Winston Churchill

Our Boston terrier, Max, was a doggie version of a Timex watch. He took lots of lickings from life, but he kept on ticking because he loved and wanted to serve his masters.

First Max's vision took a licking. Late one night one of our cats scratched Max's eye. It was bleeding, so we rushed him to the emergency vet. They treated him as best they could, and we took him to our regular vet the next day. Despite their best efforts, Max lost sight in that eye. But it didn't stop him from his guarding activities. He watched everyone who came into our driveway. If they were strangers, he let us know with an angry bark. If they were friends, he greeted them with enthusiasm.

Max took a licking on his hip. He hurt it somehow. We noticed because he started limping. Then arthritis set in. Even though it was obviously difficult for him, he'd get up and greet us whenever we came home.

At the end of his life, when Max's ticking was slowing to a stop, we carried him outside to take care of his "business." We made a bed for him by the window, near his food and water. Max still kept on keeping on until the vet told us he didn't have much left in him. He had fulfilled his duties to his masters, despite his challenges. We didn't want him to suffer, so we let the vet put him down. He lived with purpose; his life was complete. "Well done, good and faithful Max."

I've also taken some lickings in my life, but God has allowed me to keep on ticking too. I've realized that even though life has beaten me up a bit, I am still useful to my Master, and I refuse to quit.

After I had a bad car accident many years ago, I kept on ticking in ways that kept me upbeat and active. Admittedly some were inconvenient for others and may have seemed inconsequential...but not to me. I had my husband, Steve, roll me up to the choir loft in my wheelchair so I could sing in our church services. I kept on working in the church kitchen in my wheelchair, even though I may have gotten in the way a bit. Hopefully I was being strong and obedient.

After I learned to walk again, I volunteered at my children's classrooms at school and in the music department. A little later I went back to college, finished my degree, and began teaching. These were all things God had called me to do, and I wasn't going to give in to the beating my body had taken. And I believe God honored my obedience. Several months after the wreck, my doctor performed surgery on both legs to see what could be done. He told me I would be able to walk for a while, but in seven years or so I would probably be in a wheelchair for the rest of my life. That was 22 years ago—and I'm not in one yet!

My latest licking was to my ticker. I had quadruple bypass

heart surgery a few months ago. Again I was determined to persevere with the task at hand—writing this book. God gave me a heart doctor named "Dr. Paw" to comfort and encourage me... and make me smile. God was still in charge, and He certainly has a sense of humor!

Like Max, my intention is to serve my Master until the end of my life. I don't know why I was spared so many times, but I know who spared me. I'll keep on ticking for Him until He finally takes me into His presence. I want to hear His "Well done, good and faithful Connie!"

One thing I do: Forgetting what is behind and straining toward what is ahead, I press on toward the goal to win the prize for which God has called me heavenward in Christ Jesus (Philippians 3:13-14).

Consider This

What are some lickings you've taken in life? How have they affected you? How did you keep on ticking? How did God encourage you? How can you use what you've experienced to encourage someone else?

She Shall Overcome

God Lets Us Grow

Unless you try to do something beyond what you have already mastered, you will never grow.

RALPH WALDO EMERSON

The joy of Chrissy's life is Tasha, her pretty Lhasa apso rescue dog. When Tasha was 10 years old, Chrissy began to notice a dulling on her dog's normally beautiful, sparkling brown eyes. Not thinking it was serious, Chrissy procrastinated taking Tasha to the vet. When she finally did, she was told Tasha had cataracts and was blind. Surgery was a possibility, but the vet advised Chrissy to wait and see how Tasha dealt with her loss of sight. Chrissy plunged into despair at the thought that her dog would never see again.

She started coddling her "poor baby," carrying Tasha everywhere to make sure she wouldn't bump into a wall or fall off a step and hurt herself. Tasha picked up on Chrissy's heavy heart. For a while, the joyful relationship between master and dog disappeared. Then Chrissy went online and discovered a huge community of other dog owners whose pets had gone blind. The biggest lesson she learned from their collective wisdom was to not coddle or overprotect Tasha. The other pet owners advised, "Don't pick your dog up and carry it around. Blind dogs have an amazing 'God-given' ability to adapt. Let them walk around the house on their own, and they will soon figure out the lay of the land."

Chrissy realized she'd been blind too. Her perception shifted completely. She went from grief to hope as she determined to be the best master she could be. She set out to help Tasha regain the self-confidence she'd lost because of Chrissy's overprotection.

And lo and behold, as Chrissy let go to let Tasha adjust, the dog did adapt. She soon relied on her senses of smell and touch to guide her. She memorized the pattern of the house. She knew which room she was in by the feel of the different surfaces on the sensitive pads of her feet—from the smooth linoleum of the kitchen to the familiar bedroom rugs. A first-time visitor to Chrissy's home has a hard time discerning that this active, self-assured dog is blind.

Seeing how Tasha has grown in confidence and courage is a daily source of inspiration to Chrissy and a constant reminder that over-helping the ones we love may do more harm than good.

I learned this lesson with respect to my son. It's so tempting for parents to coddle their kids. I still want to tie Skye's shoes, but now he insists on doing it himself—even though he takes forever and his handiwork often comes undone in a few minutes. Only by practicing restraint does my wife allow Skye to go to the refrigerator to pour himself a glass of milk. A little boy with a carton of milk in one hand and a glass in the other always looks to her like an accident waiting to happen—and sometimes it does.

One of Skye's favorite games at age five was for me to pretend to be overprotective of him when we hiked together. We'd come to a mountain stream, and I'd tell him he couldn't cross those "surging wild waters" on his own. I'd insist I would have to pick him up and carry him across like I did when he was two. He enjoyed "defying" me, boldly proclaiming he could cross without my help. I'd get in front of him, step on a midstream rock and reach back and shout, "Take my hand or you'll fall in and be swept away!" But he'd smile and scamper over the rocks, beaming with joy at having done it on his own.

If we don't let Skye pour his own milk or tie his own shoes or do his own homework or drive his own car or choose his own profession one day, how will he grow up to become the man God designed him to be?

How does this relate to our relationship with our Father in heaven? Just as overprotectiveness can stunt the growth of a dog or a child, it can hinder a child of God. Have you ever wondered why God doesn't help you more? As humans, we often don't understand. We cry out and feel like God turns a deaf ear. We plead for intervention, wondering why He doesn't hurl down lightning bolts to destroy our enemies or send angels to carry us across a seemingly impassable obstacle. We want to be coddled, even babied—but our wise Creator allows us room to grow instead.

I can't count the number of prayers I've uttered pleading for a big breakthrough in my career. I've screamed, whispered, gotten down on my knees, lifted my hands heavenward, fasted, tithed, sang songs, memorized scriptures, built altars—everything short of killing a goat—all to get the attention of my Father "up there" whom I believe with one flick of His pinky can make me the most successful (and, at the same time, most godly) writer in the world. That's the attitude I came into the game with. But God has changed me. After 25 years of wondering why God hasn't intervened on my behalf, I realize more and more that I've been pursuing a false goal. What I perceived as God refusing to help was actually His perfect plan for helping me grow. God heard all my cries and whispers. All the time I spent in prayer and supplication was not wasted. Each day I am more grateful, more thankful, and more joyful over the epiphany that the most successful aspect of my "writing career" is that it's brought me closer to Him.

I thank God for His great wisdom to know when to lift me up and carry me across the streams of life and when to let little boys pour their own milk or tie their own shoes. He knows that sometimes the best answer to our cries and yearnings is the pure, profound silence that encourages us to be still and know Him. As we enter into His holy presence, we suddenly find all our needs met and our hearts filled with His peace that passes understanding.

So the next time you think God isn't listening, perhaps it's time to start listening for Him.

So be truly glad. There is wonderful joy ahead, even though you have to endure many trials for a little while. These trials will show that your faith is genuine. It is being tested as fire tests and purifies gold (1 Peter 1:6-7 NLT).

Consider This

Has someone overprotected or coddled you? What were the results? Do you have prayers that seem unanswered? Can you see how this might be God's wisdom?

Happy Pill
Cheering Others Serves God

*The best way to cheer yourself up is
to try to cheer somebody else up.*

Mark Twain

If God gave spiritual gifts to dogs, Cookie's gift would have been encouragement. She was a cockapoo/terrier mix who belonged to my brother Darrell Janzen, his wife, Joan, and their children, Mitch, Denay, and Kim. The whole neighborhood greeted Cookie when they passed the Janzen home. Everyone who knew her loved her because she made them happy.

Cookie liked to visit the primary school across the street where the Janzen girls went to class. The school staff knew where Cookie lived and that she wouldn't be a problem. Because she was so happy and never touched anyone or bothered the teachers, they allowed her to stay. When she passed their classrooms, the teachers waved "hello" to her. At recess the kids loved playing with Cookie.

I believe Cookie listened to children who needed a caring ear. She never scolded or judged anyone. In fact, she lifted their spirits by her very presence.

At lunch, the kids shared little bits of food with Cookie. Some parents even put special treats in their children's lunches for her. After lunch, Cookie helped the custodians by cleaning leftover food off the ground. They loved Cookie too.

Because Cookie's family fed her well, I know her trips to the school weren't just centered on food. She seemed to have a special mission in life: to spread good cheer. She loved people, they loved her, and life was good when Cookie was around. She didn't know the Bible verse "A cheerful heart is good medicine" (Proverbs 17:22), but that was how she lived. She was a "happy pill."

Like Cookie, my dad, Al Janzen, was a "happy pill" to many people. He was friendly to everyone. He never missed a chance to greet someone he knew, no matter where he was. Once when we were far away from our Bakersfield home and eating dinner in New Orleans, Dad suddenly jumped up and ran outside. He'd seen some folks he knew! They came in, joined us for dinner, and we laughed and visited.

Since he was a natural greeter, it made perfect sense that Dad was an usher in our church. He also usually sat on the right side of the church toward the back. The teenagers generally liked to sit on the right, so when adults wanted to sit in their section, Dad would graciously steer them to a place nearby. He loved the kids and wanted them to feel comfortable and like they had their own special place.

Dad never preached a sermon, but he was one reason people heard them. His love and care helped make them feel welcome so they kept coming back.

My dad was a good listener if anyone needed an ear. He was also willing to take risks to encourage others. I remember two fellows who came to him. They said one of them had bad feet and one had bad hands, but together they made one good, hard-working man. They asked Dad for a job, and he hired them. They worked hard, honestly, and happily. They gave off a feeling of gratitude and delight at actively belonging.

Dad never made any headlines. He never ran for political office. He never thought he was anyone special. But he was to his friends, his loved ones, and to God. Dad served a very special purpose in God's kingdom. He was a "happy pill" whose encouraging, friendly spirit made life's ups and downs easier to swallow—and God's love and care more real.

We need more Cookies and people like my dad in our lives. We need people who lift our spirits…and we can do that for others too.

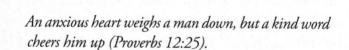

An anxious heart weighs a man down, but a kind word cheers him up (Proverbs 12:25).

Consider This

Who in your life is a "happy pill"? What about him or her most blesses and encourages you? What can you learn? How can you be more like this person?

In what ways do you tend to be hard or easy to swallow for others? If you can be a bit "crusty" at times, why is that? How can you more consistently lift other people's spirits?

I'd Rather Not Do It Myself

Stay Spiritually Fit

Laziness grows on people;
it begins in cobwebs and
ends in iron chains.

THOMAS FOWELL BUXTON

Ashley is a cream-colored schnoodle (half poodle/half schnauzer). She is bursting with life and follows her humans everywhere. But in one area, Ashley is lazy and prefers to be "done for" rather than exercise her full doggie capabilities. What doesn't Ashley like to do? Jump. Whether it's onto a couch, a bed, or into the car, she pretends she can't get there herself. She tries to coax her humans to lift her instead. But if no one's around or she spies food on a shelf, she'll jump as high as three feet for the prize...and usually gets it in one attempt! She also leaps effortlessly into the back of the family SUV when she thinks no one is looking.

Ashley's family gets a big laugh out of her efforts to "schnoodle" them. They're wise to her and don't let her laziness get out of hand. But this does raise an interesting question. What if she did manage to fool them? What if she never had to jump because they always picked her up? Would her ability to jump freely without effort gradually diminish from disuse?

I'm not sure how "use it or lose it" applies to canines, but I know what happened to my cousin's children when they were small. Suzanne was three years older than Michael and loved to carry him around. And he was very happy to let her. It wasn't until she went to preschool that Michael really started to walk on his own—because it was the first time he really had to.

My mind boggles at the implications of Michael's dependence on his sister. Just think if that had continued. What if the boy refused to walk, run, or jump on his own? If he'd hung back from learning to use his own muscles and giving them exercise, and instead settled for going only where his sister carried him, how narrow his world would have stayed! What a waste that would have been of his God-given potential.

We will also waste our God-given potential if we don't develop and exercise the spiritual muscles He's given us. One area where I've lost out by being spiritually lazy is in Bible study. When I came to know Jesus in college I met often with students who regularly studied God's Word. They lifted and carried me around when I was in the babyhood of my faith. Here and there I took a few steps on my own, but I never developed a consistent, personal habit of Bible study.

Over the years I've also sat under some wonderful pastors and Bible teachers. They brought me God's Word and fed me, just like birds feed their young. God wants all of us to get good teaching by those He has gifted that way, but if we rely on this alone, our world becomes limited. If we don't learn to dig into the Scriptures for ourselves, our spiritual dinner will be limited to what teachers set before us. And we won't be able to do what Scripture encourages us to do—to check what we're learning against God's Word (Acts 17:11).

What really jump-started my spiritual fitness in this area was joining a local Bible-study group. The class is part of a worldwide ministry designed to build each person's Bible-study "muscles." Each year classes choose a 30-week course of study from materials designed to facilitate this process and structured around a four-pronged approach I like to call the "quadruple whammy." First we study a Bible passage by ourselves. We answer questions on worksheets written to help us dig into the verses. On class day we meet in small groups and discuss our answers. Afterward, a "teaching leader" presents additional insights and reinforces what we've learned. When we go home, we study the passage one last time by reading a provided commentary on what we've covered. Then it's on to the next week's lesson.

I've been in this class for about 14 years now, and it's changed me. My perspective has flipped from human to divine. More and more I'm seeing life's ups and downs from God's point of view. My Bible study has gotten me onto my spiritual feet and provided exercise to help me walk more securely and maturely with God. As it says in Isaiah 40:30-31, "Even youths grow tired and weary, and young men stumble and fall; but those who hope in the LORD will renew their strength. They will soar on wings like eagles; they will run and not grow weary, they will walk and not be faint."

I saw this play out in my life in a very specific way when my mom passed away a year ago. I was named coexecutor of her estate. Her affairs loomed like a huge mountain threatening landslides on my head. Mom had a large home, employees, dogs, investments, and key involvements in two charities. There were also a couple of small family foundations. Mom tried to put her affairs in order, but I was faced with a host of challenges and responsibilities I'd never had to deal with before. Had I not been grounded in God's Word, had I not been building my spiritual muscles, I would not have been able to crawl through the months that followed—let alone walk with confidence in the Lord. But I understood that these new challenges were from Him. I understood He would walk with me and support me if I sought His wisdom and obeyed His leading. I understood that this was a stewardship, and that what happens in this life is "boot camp" for eternity. I knew these things because I'd been deep in His Word for years.

God wants us to be all we can be for Him. As we discover new biblical truths, our faith in and knowledge of Him will grow and we'll be better equipped to live and minister for Him and by Him.

All Scripture is God-breathed and is useful for teaching, rebuking, correcting and training in righteousness, so that the man of God may be thoroughly equipped for every good work (2 Timothy 3:16-17).

Consider This

Do you study God's Word on a consistent basis? If not, how is your lack hurting your spiritual fitness?

What is the most significant thing you've learned in your Bible study in the past year? What would you like to share most with someone else?

Birds and Music
Team with God to Do the Impossible

*A snowflake is one of God's most fragile creations,
but look what they can do when they stick together!*

AUTHOR UNKNOWN

Little John was a five-year-old purebred English pointer. He'd been at the animal shelter for over a month. His former master had dropped him off because he had to move out of state and couldn't take the dog along. Though he'd invested big bucks training Little John to be an expert hunting dog, apparently this talent wasn't in high demand in Southern California. That, coupled with the dog's age and a rumor that he'd bitten his previous owner's child, didn't make Little John a first-round draft pick.

A shelter worker became concerned about Little John's plight. She was worried that he'd be put down if he wasn't adopted soon. She called a friend who was a hunter. Mike already had a dog, but the persistent shelter worker convinced him to come down and give Little John a look. Mike wasn't sold by what he saw, but he agreed to take Little John home and give him a trial run.

Out in the wild, Little John came alive and showed Mike what an incredible hunting dog he was. Little John's senses became fully engaged in the hunt. He'd stalk out ahead of Mike. When he spotted a hidden bird, Little John would assume the "pose." His whole body would stiffen with his tail outstretched and rigid as he'd lift up one front leg and point his head directly at the prey. After Mike shot the bird, Little John would retrieve it and proudly drop the prize at his new master's feet. It was pure joy to watch.

A hunting dog needs a hunter to realize its purpose. Without Mike, Little John was just one more dog taking up kennel space. Like the old adage that says it takes two to tango, sometimes we need a partner to bring out a hidden talent we have and turn our mundane walk into glorious dancing.

When I was young, I took guitar lessons. I quickly discovered I had no affinity for music. However, I did learn a few basic chords and secretly enjoyed writing simple country-western-type songs. It was fun to talk-sing those lyrics, but making a living as a songwriter was the furthest thing from my mind.

One of my early jobs after college was writing material for a bilingual education company. While there I met an illustrator named Richard. He was concurrently writing music for a major R&B record producer. We became friends. Not being a lyricist, he eventually asked me to put words to some of his music. He liked what I wrote—and so did his boss. Next thing I knew, I was signing a contract to be a staff R&B lyricist—a position that lasted five years. Richard and I wrote more than 200 songs together. Over two dozen of them were recorded, some by Grammy-award-winning groups. I was always thrilled to hear our songs on the radio or see them charted in *Billboard Magazine*.

When I look back, I realize the impossibility of a musically challenged Chinese-American film major becoming a professional R&B lyricist. If Richard hadn't come along to be the music to my words, and if his boss hadn't given me a chance to exercise my hidden talents, I would never have gotten what became the most fun and favorite job of my youth.

Paired with Mike, Little John had the chance to reach his full hunting dog potential. Partnered with Richard, my song-writing talents could emerge. And even more than these small opportunities, God gives each one of us the ability to do impossible things by partnering with Him. Scripture gives many examples. A barren woman past the age of childbearing gives birth to a son named Isaac. A young shepherd boy fires a stone from a slingshot and fells an armor-clad Philistine giant named Goliath. An ordinary fisherman with a big mouth walks on water and becomes one of the founders of the early Christian church. You and I have no idea what we can achieve when we pair with God and let Him work through us!

In our day-to-day lives, God helps us with the impossible hurdles we encounter on the hamster wheel of life. I need to be paired up with God to give me patience when I'm trying to get a cranky little boy off to school in the morning. I need to be paired with God to trust that our family's needs will be met in the face of yet another media barrage of financial bad news. I need to be paired with God to forgive the thief who swiped my digital camera at the county fair.

Jesus said, "Here I am! I stand at the door and knock. If anyone hears my voice and opens the door, I will come in and eat with him, and he with me" (Revelation 3:20). Jesus invites us to pair with Him—now and for eternity. Who knows what we may achieve if we heed His call, leave our animal shelter existence, and follow Him?

I tell you the truth, anyone who has faith in me will do what I have been doing. He will do even greater things than these, because I am going to the Father (John 14:12).

Consider This

Have you paired up with someone who helped you fulfill some of your untapped potential? How has partnering with God helped you accomplish the impossible?

Treat

Do You Seek God or His Goodies?

I believe in the sun even if it isn't shining.
I believe in love even when I am alone.
I believe in God even when He is silent.

AUTHOR UNKNOWN

Dogs love getting goodies. That's why we use treats to train them. My youngest dog, Becca, went through an obedience course last summer. On the first day of class, her teacher showed up with a pouchful of yummies. We used the treats, along with praise, to reinforce her actions when she did what we wanted. This helped motivate her to repeat the desired behaviors.

As helpful as these treats were early in the training process, our end goal was to wean Becca off the treat reward and get her to perform for praise alone. I didn't want her to come to me or obey me just for a morsel of food. Not only would this have gotten her pudgy, it would have put our relationship on the wrong basis. I wanted Becca to obey me because she wanted to please me. I desired her greatest treat to be me! I wanted her—and my other dogs—to seek me first.

If I desire this from my dogs, how much more does my heavenly Father desire this from me? Yet to be honest, I admit I fall short. I'm much more likely to seek God out because I want something from Him than because He is my treat and I'm seeking Him first.

A dear friend I'll call Gretchen has taught me a great deal about seeking God first. She and her husband served for decades in an urban ministry. After their two older sons had a rough time in an inner-city high school, they agonized about where to send their youngest boy. Their first choice was to enroll him in a nearby parochial school. But even with the partial scholarships they'd heard they could apply for, they couldn't afford it. They felt if they couldn't find a solution they might have to leave the ministry—and they didn't feel that's what God wanted.

Gretchen went to the Lord in prayer. To her this wasn't asking for a "treat." It was pleading for a deep necessity. But God wasn't turning on a light at the end of her tunnel. She didn't know what God wanted or what she should do. Then she sensed God impressing upon her to praise Him.

Gretchen obeyed. Every day for weeks she sought out the Lord and spent time in His presence, praising and thanking Him for who He is. She read the book of Psalms and glorified God. Although nothing changed outwardly, her spirit lifted as she became overwhelmed by the knowledge of how marvelous and loving and awesome the Lord is. Oh, she still had her moments of fear. But as she sought God, her view of Him got bigger and her trust in Him was strengthened. Her problems seemed smaller by comparison. Then, out of nowhere, a friend who learned of her situation offered to provide the funds needed for her son's education!

Gretchen's son attended the parochial high school for four years and thrived.

Some years later, Gretchen and her husband faced an even

greater challenge. This time God was leading them out of the ministry where they'd spent their entire adult lives. They felt completely overwhelmed. Their ministry had supplied all their needs. Now suddenly, in their early fifties, they had to find housing, jobs, and health insurance on their own. They felt like they were jumping off a cliff with no safety net. Paralyzed and devastated, Gretchen and her husband felt led to go to God and praise Him.

This time it was much more of a struggle to seek God first, but they did. When their stress and panic rose, such as when they got yet another job rejection or they felt hurt or abandoned by someone who couldn't quite understand what they were doing, they turned to the Lord. They prayed, "Lord, we know You are in control. We know You have a plan for us even if we can't see it yet." They purposely praised Him far more than they pleaded for answers. Even when no answers from God seemed forthcoming, they delighted in and trusted Him to give them the courage to go on. They leaned on God as sheer acts of will and faith…again and again. God responded by drawing them close and restoring their joy and peace and rest despite the uncertainties that swirled around them.

God took them right down to the wire. With just one month to go before their resources ran dry, Gretchen's husband got a job. With just days to move out of their ministry quarters, God provided affordable housing. Well, almost affordable. Gretchen needed to work too, and so far she'd found nothing. They moved to their new home on faith—and a job came through soon for her also.

Gretchen and her husband sought God first when all seemed lost. So did a famous man named Job. He loved and served God, but Satan claimed this was only because God had showered Job with a multitude of "treats." Job had good health, wealth, a large and thriving family, and enormous stature in his community. Satan argued, "Stretch out your hand [God,] and strike everything he has, and he will surely curse you to your face" (Job 1:11).

So God let Satan put Job to the test.

Job lost everything—livestock, servants, children, even his health. His wife told him to curse God and die! Job despaired about his misfortunes, but he said, "As long as I have life within me...my lips will not speak wickedness" (Job 27:3-4). Ultimately he and God dialogued. Job was "treated" to an up-close-and-personal view of the Lord (Job 38–42). He stopped griping about what he'd lost, bowed before God's greatness, and repented. And God heaped more blessings on him than ever (Job 42:10-16).

When my dogs obey me and receive praise and a cuddle, when they seek to be in my presence just for me, it gladdens my heart. I believe it delights and gladdens God when we do that with Him. He is eager to draw us close and give us the very best "treats" of all—eternal love and everlasting intimacy with Him.

Delight yourself in the Lord *and he will give you the desires of your heart (Psalm 37:4).*

Consider This

Do you go to God for "treats" or to be in His presence? What do you most love and appreciate about Him? How do you express praise and thankfulness to Him daily?

Set Your Face to Go

Fix Your Heart Toward Heaven

Our plans miscarry because they have no aim.
When a man does not know what harbor
he is making for,
no wind is the right wind.

SENECA

When our children were still little I longed for a Boston terrier. I started researching and soon heard about a "runt" at a reasonable price. We drove more than 100 miles to meet her. We fell in love instantly, but she was so tiny we weren't sure she'd make it home.

Mandy did and she grew into a nice family dog. When it was time for our fishing vacation in Oregon, we didn't want to leave her with friends, so we took her along. She traveled well, and people we met along the way really enjoyed her. When we reached our destination, she found her own sleeping place by the children in our second-floor hotel room. She loved being near them, and they loved it too.

Surprisingly, Mandy loved going out on the boat with us. Our little black-and-white puppy stood quietly on the bow, seeming to search for the big catch of the day.

On one occasion, the rest of the family decided to go for a quick boat trip and leave Mandy with me in the room. Mandy sat out on the balcony for a while and then came and curled up next to me for a nap. That's where she was when she spotted my husband and children walking up the path to the hotel. She was so eager to greet them that she "set her face to go" and raced full speed out the door and off the end of the balcony. She soared approximately 20 feet. I watched in horror since there was no way I had time to stop her. Steve and the kids saw her coming, but at that point they couldn't get close enough to catch her. She landed hard and skinned her chin, but thankfully she suffered no real harm. She seemed to smile as she was comforted, lapping up the love she lived for and giving it right back.

This made me wonder, *Is that how I will be when I get to see Jesus face-to-face? When this life is over, will I be so excited to be in His presence that I'll run without concern and jump into His arms?*

That's the way my mom was. As her life drew to a close, she would wake up every morning disappointed that she hadn't yet gone to be with the Lord. There were days when she would say, in a witty kind of way, "All my brothers and sisters are going to think I didn't make it to heaven. They're all there, and I'm not."

Mom deeply loved her Lord and Savior. It was easy to see this as I was growing up. In those days, she "set her face to go" by living for Him. She was faithful to study the Bible, pray, attend church, and serve others. When she turned 90 years old, it was easy to see why her yearning to be totally in His presence grew. She wanted to leap off the balcony of this life and into His everlasting arms.

I often took Mom to lunch and frequently invited my daughter Christy along because Mom enjoyed her company. Christy had the caring granddaughter touch that made Mom smile. Mom wanted us to be with her, but she didn't want to eat. She'd say, "I just want to go!" One day, just before she died, she said, "I went to heaven. Cover me up!" She had "set her face to go." And on the day the Lord finally let her in, she looked up, smiled, closed her eyes, and went to be with Him.

The apostle Paul also loved the Lord. He said, "To me, to live is Christ and to die is gain" (Philippians 1:21). To Paul, this meant he would live his life in obedience to Christ, but when he died and passed totally into Christ's presence, that would be even more wonderful.

Mandy's whole focus was to be with her loved ones. My mom and the apostle Paul's total focus was to please Christ, to live for Him, and to enter into His presence one day. If we set our hearts on heaven and our faces toward going to Him, what will that look like in our lives?

And it came to pass, when the time was come that he should be received up, he stedfastly set his face to go to Jerusalem (Luke 9:51 KJV).

Consider This

Are you looking forward to being in Christ's physical presence? If you set your heart more on Jesus and heaven, how will that affect your life here on earth?

Boning Up II
Obedience Training

1. What advantage does renaming a dog you've just adopted have in training?

2. How does praise reinforce learning?

3. When can repetition be counterproductive?

4. What commands might save your dog's life?

5. How can you teach your puppy not to jump up on you?

Part 3

Paws for Healing
Let God Smooth Out the Tangles

BUBBA
(Before)

BUBBA
(After)

Bubba's Mystery Pounds
Will You Choose God's Truth?

Your stomach shouldn't be a waist basket.

AUTHOR UNKNOWN

Humans aren't the only ones who struggle with extra pounds. Bubba certainly did. He was a big Australian shepherd/border collie mix who belonged to my friend Susie. When he was getting older, Bubba started gaining weight. The vet told Susie she had to do something about it. If she watched what Bubba ate and made sure he got more exercise, they could get him into better health.

Susie tried. She gave Bubba the right portions of dog food. She made sure someone walked him every day. But rather than losing weight, Bubba gained pounds. This alarmed Susie, but she didn't know what to do. She tried different kinds of dog food. Bubba's weight kept rising. Susie's husband, Glen, and her older son, Monte, took Bubba for longer walks, but that didn't help either.

One day Susie was cleaning up the den, and she noticed two pizza plates on the floor. Then over the next few days she saw other wrappers, trays, and plates around. Her younger son, Grant, was obviously snacking. When she asked him about it, he told her he'd been seeing who could eat more, him or Bubba.

Grant had no intention of hurting Bubba. He just wanted to know how much food his dog could pack away. He didn't realize he was sabotaging Bubba's health. Once he understood this, Grant helped Bubba eat right and exercise. The "mystery pounds" dropped off.

Like Bubba, I've struggled with extra pounds. I've always had a weight problem. When I was in high school I thought I was terribly heavy, but I was really just a little overweight. (I'd love to be that weight now!) I put on pounds during my pregnancies, and I couldn't seem to lose them.

Finally, I went on a special weight-loss program. I was limited to 1000 calories a day. I couldn't eat any sugars or wheat products. If I cheated, even just a little, I would be kicked out of the program. I was told I'd probably stay fat for the rest of my life if I didn't follow the regimen. I did so well I lost more than 70 pounds!

But then I cheated. And I believed the program's statement that cheating meant I was doomed to failure forever. That lie sabotaged me, just like Grant had sabotaged Bubba. I gained all the weight back, and it affected my health. I suffered serious consequences because I chose to believe a lie rather than choosing to obey God and believe His truth that I could do all things through Jesus.

Grant didn't know he was hurting Bubba by disobeying the rules Susie had instituted regarding Bubba's eating. But I knew I was disobeying my Lord. I knew God cared about my health and wanted me to be at my best. The apostle Paul wrote, "Do you not know that your body is a temple of the Holy Spirit, who is in you, whom you have received from God? You are not your own; you were bought at a price. Therefore honor God with your body" (1 Corinthians 6:19-20). While the context of this statement has to do with sexual sin, I believe God wants us to take good care of our bodies because we are His, and He cares about our health.

These days I'm trying to do that. I'm choosing to believe God's truth and asking Him for wisdom to make the right food choices each day. I'm exercising the way my doctors have told me to. When I make wrong decisions or when I don't exercise as I should, I pray to my Master and ask His forgiveness...and return to my healthy eating plan.

Last week my husband, Steve, and I were on vacation. I obediently took the medication I'm on for my health. We went on long walks. But we also ate a lot of "vacation food." This gave us upset stomachs and increased our weight. So once again I asked God for guidance, and now I'm back to eating healthier. It's an ongoing battle that won't be won in a day. But God is with me all the time so there's hope!

When I think of my struggle with food, I'm encouraged by the story of Daniel. In a different way, he was challenged to obey God regarding food choices (Daniel 1). He and three other young men (Shadrach, Meshach, and Abednego) were among an elite group of exiled Jews who'd been taken to the Babylonian court. They were offered royal food and wine that didn't conform to Jewish dietary laws. Eating this food and drinking this wine meant disobeying God's commands. So they asked the king's representative if they could eat only vegetables and drink water. The guard appointed over them agreed to let them try it for ten days to make sure their health wouldn't deteriorate. God rewarded their obedience. They thrived on the diet, and God granted them great wisdom, knowledge, and understanding. As a result, they found favor at court and entered the king's service.

Susie loved Bubba and helped him get healthy. God wants to

do the same for me. He will give me what I need to obey Him for my benefit—if I rely on Him.

♣ ♣

Meanwhile [Jesus'] disciples urged him, "Rabbi, eat something."
But he said to them, "I have food to eat that you know nothing about."
Then his disciples said to each other, "Could someone have brought him food?"
"My food," said Jesus, "is to do the will of him who sent me and to finish his work" (John 4:31-34).

Consider This

Have you given in to a lie because it was easier to believe than obeying God's truth? What were the consequences? Is this happening to you right now? How can you change this and obey God's truth for your good?

When Old Tapes Play
Past Hurts Need Healing

One need not be a chamber to be haunted,
one need not be a house;
the brain has corridors surpassing
material place.

EMILY DICKINSON

My dog Morgan was spooked. Kyle, my friend's son, was jumping around in "rock star mode" as he played a popular video game in my den. My little dog didn't realize this behavior was harmless. Somewhere back in my dog's early life, before I had him, he'd either been abused or suffered an awful fright. Even though he's been mine for ten years, whatever he went through is still buried in his subconscious. Something about Kyle's antics, or maybe the game's loud music, or both, set Morgan off. He saw Kyle as a threat and barked stridently at the boy.

Now it was Kyle's turn to be spooked. He had some "old tapes" of his own. As a toddler, he'd been chased and knocked down by two huge dogs. They hadn't bitten him, but he'd been scraped up by his fall. He's feared dogs ever since. Kyle had been around our house enough to know Morgan, and the boy normally just kept his distance or ignored the dog altogether. Morgan's aggressive reaction changed that. Kyle gasped "Whoa!" and backed away, looking nervous.

Fortunately, I was right there to intervene and calm dog and boy. Then I seized the chance to help build a little insight. I wanted Kyle to realize he and Morgan had something important in common.

"Kyle, you know how you had a bad experience with dogs when you were young?" I asked. "Well, when Morgan was young, he had a bad experience with humans. Sometimes something triggers those memories. When you jumped around, it scared him."

Morgan and Kyle aren't alone in reacting to current situations based on old hurts that haven't fully healed. I think to varying degrees, we all do that. But if we're alert and aware and seek the Lord when these triggers are pulled, I believe God can use such episodes for healing.

One of my old emotional hurts focuses around rejection from boys. In grade school I was rather socially awkward. I was also on the chunky side. I got teased a lot by the boys in my class. It hurt. But it wasn't what hurt most. The most painful events were the ballroom dancing classes on Friday afternoons after school. The entire sixth grade attended. For me it was "Ego Smashing 101." The most popular girls danced with boys. The rest of us danced with each other, alone, or sat on the sidelines.

At year's end, we had one final dance. Partway through an extremely popular boy approached me. He invited me to dance with him. I couldn't handle it. I was tongue-tied and had two left feet. His 11-year-old ego could only stand the embarrassment for so long. He left me standing in the middle of the floor and stepped out with one of the most popular girls in school. I did what any sensible female would—I ran into the bathroom and cried.

Over the years relationships got a bit better between boys and me—especially after I came to know Jesus in college. Now I had "brothers in Christ" who took time to care about me. But the "ugly duckling rejection tapes" remained, and they could be triggered by relatively innocent events.

One such triggering incident happened when I was around 30. I was living and working in Los Angeles. One day I went to lunch with friends from a church career singles group. A female pal was getting a lot of attention from the men among us. I started feeling like a reject. The intellectual part of my brain told me I was overreacting, but my emotions were right back on that sixth-grade dance floor.

When I was safely home by myself, I had a good cry—as I had years before. But God was gracious and used that episode for healing. I realized my feelings were just that—*feelings*. I also realized it was okay to have them, and that they didn't represent the reality of what had just happened.

Recently a dear friend experienced a similar feeling of abandonment. The small church she'd loved and served in for more than 20 years disbanded. Most of her friends found new church homes, but family considerations caused her to postpone her own decision. This was getting her down. "I feel so left out," she told me. Then she explained that she'd been left out a lot as a kid, and this situation was triggering "old tapes." My dear friend and Bible teacher then confirmed that God takes us back through old hurts we might not wish to revisit to complete His healing work.

Many centuries ago an Old Testament prophet named Jeremiah suffered huge rejection and persecution from his people. God commanded him to give His people a message of judgment (unpopular, obviously), and he obeyed. He was persecuted because of it. His memory banks were filled with pain. Nonetheless, he held fast to the Lord. Jeremiah wrote,

I remember my affliction and my wandering, the bitterness and the gall. I well remember them, and my soul is downcast within me. Yet this I call to mind and therefore I have hope: Because of the LORD's great love we are not consumed, for his compassions never fail. They are new every morning; great is your faithfulness (Lamentations 3:19-23).

No matter what affliction we've suffered, no matter what fear and hurt lie buried in our memory banks, God is greater. If we give our pain to Him, He will lift us and heal us with His everlasting love.

I waited patiently for the LORD; he turned to me and heard my cry. He lifted me out of the slimy pit, out of the mud and mire; he set my feet on a rock and gave me a firm place to stand. He put a new song in my mouth, a hymn of praise to our God. Many will see and fear and put their trust in the LORD (Psalm 40:1-3).

Consider This

Do you have "old tapes" of past hurts in your memory? What are they? What triggers them now? How are you tempted to react?

Have you turned to the Lord for healing? If yes, how has He helped you? If not, why not talk to Him today about your pain?

The Dog That Prayed
Receive God's Answer

The value of consistent prayer is not
that He will hear us, but that we will hear Him.

WILLIAM McGILL

Pastor John loves raising beautiful black Labrador retrievers. Abigail fit the description magnificently. She was gorgeous, smart, loving, and attentive. John had a great time training her. She learned how to come, sit, stay, fetch, and play doggie games. John's favorite was teaching her to pray.

Abigail's trick was an enjoyable way to share prayer with children. Before John came to our congregation, he was a pastor at a church that had a school. I taught there at the same time. For a special chapel service, John would bring Abigail up to the stage. He would show her a cookie and then put his arm out. She would sit up and put both paws on his arm and lay her head down between them as if praying. When John said "Amen," Abigail would look up and gratefully receive her cookie. Everyone was delighted with Abigail's performance and her willingness to stay "in prayer" until John said, "Amen." They cheered when she finally got her cookie.

But John's presentation wasn't done yet. Abigail took medication for a thyroid condition. John would have her get in the prayer position and then show her the blue pill. With great fervor, she'd turn her nose up and look away. She didn't want what was good for her.

John used this very fun and interesting visual aid to enlighten the children about the importance of receiving God's answers to prayer. Abigail didn't want the blue pill, but her master knew what was best for her. Abigail had to obey in the end. And because she took the pill, she remained healthy. Have you experienced something similar with God?

Watching Abigail submit to John and bow for prayer was really sweet and touched many lives. But her refusal to joyfully accept the blue pill because it wasn't her desire was a profound lesson in itself.

There have been times in John's life when he didn't want to take a "blue pill." He wanted his prayers answered his way. When he was going to seminary, God took him out of school for two and a half years. This wasn't the answer to prayer John wanted, but God was refining him and preparing him for future ministry. What seemed a bitter pill at the time proved to be just the spiritual medicine John needed to keep his life and ministry healthy.

In the Bible, Jesus taught His disciples—and us!—how to pray. We call it the Lord's Prayer:

> Our Father in heaven, hallowed be your name, your kingdom come, your will be done on earth as it is in heaven. Give us today our daily bread. Forgive us our debts, as we also have forgiven our debtors. And lead us not into temptation, but deliver us from the evil one (Matthew 6:9-13).

Jesus demonstrated prayer and talked about it with His disciples. Just before He was arrested, Jesus prayed, "Father, if you are willing, take this cup from me; yet not my will, but yours be done" (Luke 22:42).

John shared this example in our church, teaching people that prayer isn't saying "not God's will but mine." Rather, it's "not my will but God's." It involves submitting our lives to our heavenly Father, knowing that His answers to prayer aren't always what we ask for, but they are *always* what is best for us.

This is the confidence we have in approaching God: that if we ask anything according to his will, he hears us (1 John 5:14).

Consider This

Have you had God answer a prayer in a way you didn't like? Did you "turn your head away"? What was the result? What did you learn?

Is there an area where God is asking you to pray "not my will but Yours" right now?

Truth from Tangles
God Grooms Our Hearts

*To be humbly ashamed is to be plunged
in the cleansing bath of truth.*

GEORGE MACDONALD

When we first took Squitchey into our home, grooming the little Yorkshire terrier mix was at the top of our "must do" list. She was cute and darling, but her coat was dirty and stringy. Though she was happy overall, she seemed a bit shy. We thought maybe this was due to her unkempt appearance. We tried to brush her, and she sat still for this, but there were tangles we just couldn't handle.

After showing Squitchey around her new home, we decided to give her a bath. She sat and let the warm water run over her. Her appearance was greatly improved as the dirt and grime washed off. Being cleaned up seemed to lift her spirits as well.

This was all fine, but Squitchey still needed the stubborn tangles combed out. We asked our vet to suggest a professional groomer. His office recommended one, so off Squitchey and I went. When we arrived at the nice shop, I told the lady what I wanted done. I held Squitchey in my arms and petted her. I told her I'd be back for her soon. Squitchey seemed fine, but when I walked out I felt like I was leaving my baby in the nursery for the first time.

As I was driving back to the groomer's, I wondered how Squitchey had been acting. Had she gotten scared and caused a ruckus? They hadn't phoned me, so I hoped everything was okay. I heard low growling and high-pitched whining when I entered the shop, just what I might expect to hear in a dog salon. Then I saw Squitchey. She was sitting quietly, as if posing for a picture. She even seemed to smile. Someone lifted her out of her cage. Everyone said goodbye to her as if she was their cherished queen. She kept her regal demeanor while they handed her to me, as if she were presiding over the royal changing of the guard.

Just like proper physical grooming made all the difference to Squitchey, spiritual untangling has made a huge difference in my life. I badly needed it following a serious car wreck. My legs were severely injured, and I spent months at home in bed. One day, I put my wheelchair in the back of our van and went to the mall by myself for the first time. I needed to prove to myself I could go there without the help of my husband and children.

As I was pushing my wheelchair along, using it as a walker, I started feeling sorry for myself. I grumbled about how unfair life was. It wasn't right that my family's life had been altered in such a terrible way. And it was even worse for me. *Poor, poor me,* I thought. *No one understands my pain.* Tears fell and my posture slumped.

Then God took me to the groomer's.

As I made my way down the mall, I saw someone coming toward me—a man in a wheelchair. He had no legs. He was wheeling his chair with his arms, appearing to be using all the strength he had. I stopped and watched him, and I suddenly realized how thoughtless and selfish I'd been. I was choosing to stay in the mud of self-pity, all matted up with anger and defeat. But my time in the wheelchair was going to be short compared to his. And I would definitely walk again.

As the man passed, he looked up at me. Our eyes met with understanding. As he went on his way, I watched him and prayed. I asked the Lord to bless him the way I was blessed. I asked my heavenly Father to forgive my bad attitude and negative thoughts.

I knew how Squitchey felt all these years later because back at that mall I felt clean and happy and well-groomed. Pushing the chair wasn't such a big deal anymore.

We groom Squitchey because she's ours, and we love her and care about her. God grooms me because I am His beloved child. I'm grateful that He is freeing me of my spiritual dirt and tangles so I can look and feel like the daughter of my King.

❖ ❖

Let us draw near to God with a sincere heart in full assurance of faith, having our hearts sprinkled to cleanse us from a guilty conscience and having our bodies washed with pure water (Hebrews 10:22).

Consider This

What are some spiritual mats and tangles in your life? Have you been letting the Lord groom them out? If not, why not? If so, what benefits has this brought?

Doggie 911
What's Your Spiritual Diagnosis?

*In order to change, we must be
sick and tired of being sick and tired.*

AUTHOR UNKNOWN

I was alarmed by the phone call I'd just received about Pixie, my mom's beloved 11-year-old Peke-a-poo. He'd been refusing food and couldn't stand up. I was shocked. I'd seen him a couple of days before, and he'd seemed fine. Clearly he was in dire trouble now.

Since Mom's death, Pixie had been staying at her house with the property's caretakers, who promised to take good care of him. I thought he'd do best there while I looked for a permanent new home for him. I lived an hour and a half away, so I asked my employees to step in on this emergency. "Take him straight to the vet," I urged, "and have him call me."

Over the next few hours the doctors at the excellent veterinary clinic examined Pixie and ran tests. It turned out he had beginning pneumonia. They started him on antibiotics and sent him home. I was puzzled about how this could have happened and wondered if the house was being kept too cold. Perhaps, the vets said, but they had another idea. They'd noticed Pixie had dental problems. The source of his pneumonia might be an infection in his mouth. If we were to keep him healthy, we needed to attack the problem at its source.

Once the pneumonia was safely gone, we did just that. A vet at the clinic cleaned Pixie's mouth and pulled the infected teeth. After a recovery period, Pixie was good to go. Meanwhile, a cousin of mine agreed to take him. Now Pixie is happy and healthy and thriving with his loving new family. Finding the root cause of his illness made all the difference to Pixie's health and well-being.

My friend Craig also had symptoms that started suddenly and required a skilled diagnosis to keep him out of serious trouble. He first noticed something amiss on a Friday afternoon when he was playing basketball with his young son. He felt a numbness on the bottoms of his toes. As the weekend progressed, his fingertips went numb. The tip of his tongue soon felt numb and tingly, and he lost his sense of taste. Then the numbness in his toes spread. It worked its way up to his knees, and by Monday he was numb up to the waist. He also heard ringing in his ears.

Craig's doctor knew there was more than one possible cause of his symptoms, and it was crucial to identify the right culprit. He sent Craig for a CAT scan and an MRI. He also had Craig's spinal fluid tested. It turned out Craig had a relatively rare autoimmune ailment known as Guillain-Barré syndrome. The body's immune system goes out of whack and attacks its own nervous system.

Symptoms, severity, and recovery time vary widely with Guillain-Barré syndrome, but it can be life-threatening. One of the possible effects is paralysis of the respiratory muscles. The right diagnosis and care is crucial. Craig's numbness spread to his chest and his breathing went down by 25 percent. But by then he was admitted to the hospital where they could monitor him. Thankfully, his case proved relatively mild. His breathing normalized in a few days, and he was released. Most of his symptoms subsided within three to six months. But even now, two years later, he notices a slight distortion in the feeling on the bottoms of his feet.

Finding the root cause of our ills is also crucial to our spiritual well-being. I've seen this operate in my own life with regard to guilt. I'm the hyper-responsible child of hyper-responsible parents. I'm the kid who wondered when my mom had a miscarriage if my misbehavior helped cause it. I was and am the person who thinks that when anything goes wrong around me, it must be my fault. Okay, so I had a Jewish mother. But I can't lay my whole guilt complex at the feet of that stereotype. I guess I'm just wired this way.

When I asked Jesus into my heart, I was told my sins were forgiven. I learned that my genuine guilt had been paid for on the cross. God had dealt with my spiritual infection, and He would continue to cleanse and heal me as I kept confessing my sins to Him. I also learned that Satan would try to paralyze me with "false guilt" or feelings of not being forgiven. I learned this—but I still have trouble telling the two kinds of guilt apart. When my spiritual immune system (conscience) turns on me without good cause, I need my Great Physician to treat my guilt hang-ups—and He does.

Pixie and Craig are healthy today because they got the right medical care. I'm getting healthier as God cares for me. Through His Spirit, His Word, and His people, God continues His healing work so I can stay spiritually fit in Him.

Praise the LORD, O my soul, and forget not all his benefits—who forgives all your sins and heals all your diseases, who redeems your life from the pit and crowns you with love and compassion, who satisfies your desires with good things so that your youth is renewed like the eagle's (Psalm 103:2-5).

Consider This

How would you rate your spiritual health? Are there matters that could benefit from careful diagnosis? Have you asked God to reveal any sickness or unhealthiness through His Word, His Spirit, or His people? If He has, are you willing to submit to His treatment?

Puppy Beware
Get Your Spiritual Shots

Caution is the eldest child of wisdom.

Victor Hugo

Brody was only six weeks old when my sister Tami and her husband, Raul, brought him home. The purebred German shepherd puppy wouldn't finish getting all his puppy shots until he was four months old. Brody's breeder made it clear that in the meantime he should be kept from exposure to the germs he wasn't immunized against yet.

Tami and Raul transformed their kitchen into a comfortable nest for their rambunctious little guy, complete with a sheepskin bed and plenty of chew toys. They plugged all the holes in their backyard fence and never left Brody unsupervised for fear he might get loose. They didn't take him out on walks because one casual sniff or careless lick where other dogs had been could result in serious sickness. Even though Brody was brimming with boundless puppy energy and curiosity, he wasn't allowed to explore beyond the set boundaries or play with others of his kind. His humans had to make him wait until he was vaccinated—until his immune system was strong enough to resist and fight whatever germs came his way.

Just as Brody's masters needed to protect him against dangers he was too young to handle, so human parents have a duty to protect their children. My son, Skye, is seven years old now. He's innocent. He still loves his stuffed dog and is fascinated by roly-poly bugs. He looks forward to trips to the county fair. His mom and I have a duty to guard him from things that would damage his tender psyche. We decide what "things of the world" are age-appropriate and healthy for him and what is mental, physical, or spiritual junk food.

If we're driving in the car and the radio news is especially grim, we'll turn it off. If he wants to see a movie, we read reviews and check ratings first. If the film contains images or storylines we don't think are good for our son, we say no. We supervise Skye's computer time and don't let him play violent or morally questionable video games—even if he throws a tantrum in protest. We are careful about what music he listens to and what books and magazines he reads. It's a 24/7 job to protect the heart and soul of a little kid in today's world, but that's our responsibility as his parents.

Just as Brody needed vaccinations to boost his physical immunities, so Skye needs to be inoculated with positive values. We know we only have a relatively short time to accomplish this. Soon he'll grow up, venture outside our "backyard," and make his own choices. Hopefully his spiritual "immune system" will be strong enough by then to keep him safe.

It's not only kids like Skye who need protection. So do those who are "babes in Christ." Even though we may be worldly wise adults, highly regarded in our professions, and pillars of our communities, when we first come to know the Lord our spiritual immune systems aren't fully developed. We're at risk from spiritual diseases and the temptations that are all around us. We need time to be vaccinated with God's truth. While that's happening we need the spiritual equivalent of a backyard fence or parental boundaries to keep us safe. Healthy boundaries may come in the form of a Christ-centered church, a Spirit-filled Bible study, or discipleship by a mature Christian.

I didn't have this protection for a while after I was first introduced to Christ. Because I only went to church occasionally and didn't interact closely with other believers, I was highly susceptible to worldly temptations and moral infections. A recent USC film school grad, I was mainly concerned with two things: getting an industry job and having fun. I sent out what seemed like 5000 resumes and query letters—but after six months, I hadn't gotten a single bite. In desperation I applied for waiter and sign painter jobs. But I still didn't get any nibbles.

Peggy, another recent college grad who was more mature in the Lord than I was, saw my despair. She knew I needed to spend time in a fenced yard. She invited me to attend a weekend church retreat in the mountains. I wasn't thrilled about giving up a weekend of partying to hang out with a bunch of Christians, but she was insistent. She believed I needed to get away from the world, be nurtured by strong believers, and get inoculated with a concentrated dose of God's Word, prayer, and worship.

During the retreat I stayed skeptical, declining to take in any solid spiritual food. I asked questions like, "What happens to Buddhists who live incredibly kind and unselfish lives yet never hear the Word? What about the ancient Chinese who were never witnessed to? Are you saying God sends people like that to hell if they don't believe in Jesus?" When pressed about my own faith, I said I believed in Christ "just in case He's real so at least I'll go to heaven."

On the last day, Peggy asked if I had any prayer requests. I said I'd like a job—one that paid money. She asked me to pray out loud and ask God directly. If God answered, would I consider the possibility that there was more to Christianity than met my heretofore undeveloped baby Christian eyes?

It seemed ludicrous that I could ask God for something like that. Didn't He have better things to do? Like cure cancer or bring about world peace? But I agreed to pray, and so we did. There were no fireworks, voices from heaven, or a hand materializing and writing on the wall. But the next morning I got a call from Warner Brothers Studios. Would I be available to work—today?

The caller didn't see my mouth drop open to the size of a manhole cover. I reported to their accounting department. I joyously stuffed envelopes for two-and-a-half glorious days. Because I worked with such gusto, they hired me to fill in for the copier lady, who was on vacation. I eventually got a full-time job in the story department.

Getting a paying foot in the door at a studio was nice. Getting a foot in the door to heaven was a miracle. As a spiritual infant in Christ, I didn't know God would really hear all my cries and prayers. Because Peggy put me in a place of safety where I could get a "shot" of spiritual instruction, my eyes were opened to the love and care of God. I became receptive to entering His yard and submitting to further teaching and correction.

Brody may never understand that his masters fenced him in for his own good. I hope Skye will someday realize that the restrictions his mom and I placed on him—however painful for the moment—were out of love. God loves His babes infinitely more than we love our pets and children. That's why He restrains and instructs and corrects us. He wants to protect us and keep us healthy, strong, and growing in Him.

Blessed is the man whom God corrects; so do not despise the discipline of the Almighty (Job 5:17).

Consider This

Did your parents protect you by setting boundaries for you? What were they? Did they save you from danger?

Has the Lord's instruction and correction protected you? How? What can you do to protect those in your charge (human and animal)?

Motel Bark

Let God Adjust Your Volume

The cyclone derives its powers from
a calm center. So does a person.

Norman Vincent Peale

Mandy, our Boston terrier, was the runt of the litter and had a difficult beginning. She was so tiny when she came to us that when her tummy got heavy from eating she would fall into her bowl. At home she was pretty quiet. She played, ate, and slept. Nothing seemed to bother or excite her all that much.

This changed when we took her to Oregon on our vacation.

Mandy was still a puppy, but she'd gotten bigger, weighing about eight pounds. While we were driving, she slept. She would often sleep in our daughter Christy's lap. I think the pup chose Christy because of her quiet spirit. When we got to the motel, Mandy got excited because the kids played with her. She ran in circles and barked loudly, which we knew would annoy those around us. Our solution? We taught her to bark quietly. When she started getting loud, we would put our fingers to our mouths as if to say "Shhh!" Then we'd tell her in a low voice, "Mandy, motel bark." She would immediately start barking softly so that only those in our room could hear her. We thought it was a miracle, and we loved it!

Mandy grew up on that vacation, and she always remembered her "motel bark" training. When we took her to my mom's house and she'd get excited, we'd say, "Mandy, motel bark," and she would immediately change her attitude. This also happened when I took her to church for a Vacation Bible School skit. Some of the children were being noisy, and Mandy joined in. I said, "Mandy, motel bark," and she calmed down instantly. The kids were so impressed that they calmed down as well.

I confess I used to have a barking problem too. Sometimes it was a whining bark. Sometimes it was an angry, frustrated, or tired bark. My attitude was made worse by not knowing how to turn people down graciously when they asked me to help with something. There were times when I was teaching Sunday school, singing in the choir, working in the church kitchen, being a room mother at the public school, coaching students in speech, and being a wife and mother. These were all good activities, but they took too much time away from our family and my other duties.

The stress was overwhelming. As the pressure level rose, my bark (complaining) became louder. Close friends saw what my problem was. They tried to teach me to say no. It was hard, but I eventually learned. Toning down my schedule released some tension, and my loud, annoying bark became a more relaxed sigh or "motel bark."

Loud barking is often more harmful than helpful. Kids get used to it and shrug it off. Husbands learn to ignore it. Friends shy away from it. Strangers who could be future friends run from it. So how can loud barking be pleasing to God? I had to ask, "With all my projects and running around, am I accomplishing more for the Lord or less?" I gave this matter a lot of prayer and worked on my "motel bark."

These days, even when I'm alone, I relieve stress differently. I used to get into the car, roll up the windows, and bark at the top of my lungs. Now I hop into the car, close the doors and windows, and shout "Hallelujah!" This makes me smile every time...and it relieves the tension. And I think God enjoys it too!

The meek [motel barkers] will inherit the land and enjoy great peace (Psalm 37:11).

Consider This

Do you have a "barking" problem when you get stressed? How do others react? Is your Master asking you to find your "motel bark"? What can you do to give things to the Lord, relieve your tension, and find your "motel bark" faster?

Peace Dog
Be God's Instrument of Peace

*Am I not destroying my enemies when
I make friends of them?*

ABRAHAM LINCOLN

When I prayed with my dear friend Vilma about a pet for her family, we didn't know God was going to give them a "peace" dog. In fact, Vilma wasn't sure if she wanted a dog at all. Her young daughter had been begging for one, but a dog was a big commitment, and her family didn't seem in the best shape for something so momentous. I suggested she think about getting a cat instead, and we spoke to God about it together. "Lord, show me," she prayed.

Hours later Vilma met Nugget at a local animal shelter.

Nugget was a three-year-old bichon frise/poodle mix. Even though he was shaking in fear, he still let Vilma hold him. This reminded her of her fearful, yet trusting relationship with God. She felt herself relaxing—and felt him relax too. Nugget gave her peace and touched her heart, and she knew she had to take him home.

Over the next days and weeks, Nugget brought the whole family peace and created togetherness in a variety of ways. Vilma's children had been born eight years apart. Her teenage son didn't have much in common with his six-year-old sister...until Nugget came. Now their mutual love for their dog brought them closer together. Nugget also curled up between the boy and his dad when they were on their computers. And it was Nugget who triggered group hugs when he joined his people on the living room couch.

Nugget's pure heart and love touched Vilma's husband deeply and brought out his tender side. He grew softer with family members. He became more relaxed and peaceful, and when he met neighbors while walking his dog he was more social and friendly.

Nugget has brought calm in other ways too. Both Vilma and her son have been going through hormonal changes. When their emotional ups and downs due to premenopause or puberty hit at the same time, Nugget has a quiet, comforting effect. He also helps diffuse the tension in the air since Vilma's mother suffered a health crisis and came to live with them. Everyone gets along better now that Nugget is around.

Like Vilma's family, mine had a nonhuman peacemaker when I was growing up. In our case it was a "peace" bird. Pico was a mynah bird we got when I was 14. He hated discord and knew just how to filibuster for peace. His cage was next to the kitchen table, a frequent family gathering place. When I was having a "teenage moment" with my parents, he'd cut in with a shrill "a-wa-wa-wa-wa-wa." Whether it was due to his noise or our laughter, the discord usually stopped.

Nugget's peacemaking wasn't intentional—it was a by-product of his sweet nature. I'm not sure what triggered Pico's efforts. Maybe he just didn't like raised voices or our argumentative tone disturbed him. In any case, no one told Nugget or Pico to be peacemakers. But God tells us to take on this role. Jesus said, "Blessed are the peacemakers, for they will be called sons of God" (Matthew 5:9). Part of what this means for me is being less selfish. When life is all about me, I often disturb the peace unintentionally. That's what happened recently between me and a coauthor.

Connie and I were working on a children's book proposal for our publisher. My friend is a mom, a grandma, and a wonderfully creative and experienced schoolteacher. Though I've written for kids, my hands-on experience with them is limited to borrowing other people's children. Still, when I team with other writers for a project, I usually do the last editing pass, and the proposal for this children's book was no exception. I felt a portion of Connie's sample story wasn't working, so I took it out.

When I emailed Connie my edits, she disagreed with my changes. Though the hour was late, we got on the phone. She felt the deleted material should be restored. "Marion, think like a kid," she pleaded. But at that moment I was more concerned with my own agenda, and I wanted to get that project off my desk. I argued, trying to override her objections. Finally I pointed out this was just a proposal. We could always change things back later. She gave in, but I knew she wasn't happy.

The Holy Spirit wasn't happy either. I'd damaged not just my peace with Connie, but my peace with God. His Spirit nagged at my soul to reconsider. Much as I longed to send that proposal scooting through cyberspace to the publisher, God said no. I knew that though Connie had capitulated, there wasn't true harmony between us. Deep in my heart, I knew things often look different to me in the morning. Though I struggled, I finally bowed to God's prompting and decided to wait until morning before doing anything further.

The next morning I read Connie's material with rested eyes and my firing-on-all-cylinders brain. I knew instantly I'd been wrong.

I restored the deleted portion, made a few other minor changes, and emailed it to her for approval.

This time Connie was genuinely pleased. When I asked for her forgiveness, she was gracious and immediately gave it. True peace was restored because I obeyed the Lord, valued Connie's concerns and opinion, and humbled myself before both of them.

Jesus accomplished the toughest peacemaking assignment of all. By His death for our sins, He made peace between us and God. If we have His attitude and humble ourselves like He did, we too can be instruments of peace.

The wisdom that comes from heaven is first of all pure; then peace-loving, considerate, submissive, full of mercy and good fruit, impartial and sincere. Peacemakers who sow in peace raise a harvest of righteousness (James 3:17-18).

Consider This

Are you in conflict with anyone right now? How can you promote peace between you? What scriptures will give you strength and help?

The Not-So-Great Escape
Boundaries Protect Us

Boundaries are to protect life,
not to limit pleasures.

Edwin Louis Cole

My husband's sister, Chris, had two basset hounds. Jackson was fairly tame. Willie wasn't. Though he eventually learned to walk on a leash, sit, and come when called, if Willie saw a chance to escape into the wonderful world beyond the front door or garage door, he seized the opportunity and made a dash for it. That propensity to escape earned him the nickname "Wild Willie."

Anytime people came to the house to do yard work, repair work, and so forth, Chris warned them to make sure gates and doors were closed at all times. She'd leave a leash out "just in case" Wild Willie escaped. Most of them laughed at the thought of a basset hound racing off and being hard to catch. Numerous gardeners and handymen soon learned the hard way that there is more to bassets than meets the eye.

Chris remembers one especially funny incident. Her neighbor Kent had a house-painting business. He and his crew were hired to paint the inside of Chris' home. They got the usual speech about Willie's knack for escaping, and Chris left a leash by the front door. Kent and his guys just laughed. They doubted two basset hounds would be a problem.

The paint crew arrived around seven o'clock one morning. Chris was getting ready for work, and she had Willie and Jackson in the bedroom with her. She intended to let them out into the backyard before she left. Her yard was fenced into two separate areas—one for the pool and one for the dogs. Kent was refinishing the front door and had it wide open. He'd also opened the back patio door for extra ventilation. When Chris let the dogs out, Willie dashed back inside through the patio door, raced straight past a stunned Kent, and headed out the front door to freedom as fast as he could. Kent said later it was like watching a Scud missile coming at him. He didn't know a basset hound could move that fast. He now calls the wayward basset "Willie the Bullet."

Willie didn't realize that escaping the boundaries of his house and yard was dangerous for him. He was just eager and curious and out for fun. The same was true of a little boy who could have been named "Ross the Bullet."

Ross was the youngest son of some friends we spent time with when we were first married. This particular little boy was as prone to escaping as Wild Willie was. Ross could sneak away from any adult. Before anyone was aware that he was gone, he would be out of sight.

On one particular Sunday we had gone to our friends' home for dinner. We were enjoying the meal and the company when suddenly Ross' mom asked, "Where's Ross?" No one knew. Everyone jumped up to look. Finally Ross' dad yelled, "He's next door... on the roof!"

Ross had launched like a rocket and landed on the neighbor's roof. Just like Willie, he escaped his boundaries without realizing his danger. He wasn't running away or being mean or malicious. He was just being himself. Ross' dad told him to wait and hold still. He climbed up on the roof and helped his young son down.

Though you wouldn't think it from my short, round body, there are times in my life when I've been "Connie the Bullet." I've escaped boundaries too. The main boundary I flee is posted speed limits on streets and highways. Like Ross and Willie, I don't mean any harm. I'm just looking for fun and adventure and a quick arrival time.

I got my love of speed from my dad. I loved riding with him when he drove fast. It added excitement to my otherwise normal, somewhat mundane life. When I started driving, there were times when I liked to speed too.

Years ago my husband and I bought a used 1978 Jaguar. I'd been to a teachers' convention with a group of friends, and we were carpooling home. I was driving my Jag, which was new to me. I saw a friend's car pulling up beside me in the next lane. I decided to start what looked to be a great competition. We raced each other for several miles down a long and somewhat narrow road. Then I looked down and saw I was still running in first gear. I still wasn't used to shifting, so my car was getting too hot. I immediately stopped the race, and both cars pulled over so my vehicle could cool down. Everyone was laughing and joking.

Looking back, the truth is that I put my friends in danger. Both drivers exceeded the legal speed limits—boundaries put in place so we—and those around us—would stay safe. I could have collided with my friend's car, lost control of mine, or hit someone else. Thankfully, like Willie and Ross, no harm came to us...that time. And now my concern for my grown children when they drive reminds me how important it is to respect the speed limits that are put in place for our collective good.

Just as boundaries are critical for dogs and little boys and middle-aged hot-rod mamas, they are crucial for children of God. Our Father gives us His Word to keep us safe. His commands are the doors and fences and speed limits that can protect us from dangers we may not even realize are around us. While it may look like fun to run, why not avoid what could turn out to be a not-so-great escape and stay in God's yard, enjoying His love and provision?

Your word is a lamp to my feet and a light for my path. I have taken an oath and confirmed it, that I will follow your righteous laws (Psalm 119:105-06).

Consider This

Have you "escaped" into danger by crossing a boundary "just for fun"? What happened? What did you learn? Have you ever run out of God's yard and into a not-so-great escapade? What were the results? Have you come back inside?

Handle with Care
Be Tender Just as God Is

When we honestly ask ourselves which person
in our lives means the most to us,
we often find that it is those who,
instead of giving advice, solutions, or cures,
have chosen rather to share our pain and
touch our wounds with a warm and tender hand.

HENRI NOUWEN

Morgan is wounded. My little athlete who used to leap onto garden walls, climb into trees, and scale wire fences now has to work to jump onto my bed. Sometimes when I move his little body even slightly he lets out a squeal of pain. I didn't fully appreciate the gravity of his situation...until one particular day when he was so tender he would barely budge. I decided it was time to take him to the vet.

My little dog had problems before, and so I thought this time he might have aggravated an old injury that flared up from time to time. But it was much more serious than that. The vet told me Morgan had degenerative back disease. Surgery wasn't indicated yet, but it might be in the future. For now a cortisone shot would relieve his symptoms.

Morgan's doctor also warned me that I was adding to his pain by the way I handled him. My little guy loves to be in my lap, so when he'd put his front paws on me, I'd often lean down and lift him by his front legs (close to his body). The vet said to never pick him up that way again. It put pressure right where Morgan could stand it the least. In fact, the doctor said it wasn't good to lift any dog like that. But in Morgan's case, because of his bad back, it hurt him even more.

These days I handle Morgan with a lot more care. I put one hand around his middle and the other under his little rear. That way when I lift him, he is properly supported and doesn't experience additional pain.

Tender care isn't needed just for physical problems like Morgan has. It's also needed for emotional hurts. As a teen I often pushed buttons that hit my mother's emotional wounds. I was a "daddy's girl" and obviously favored him over her. We'd all be sitting at dinner, and I'd ask his opinions on things and shut Mom down when she jumped in. Because she experienced painful rejection as a child from her stepmother, in retrospect I'm sure my behavior hurt her very deeply. Dad tried to get me to be more sensitive, but I wasn't terribly receptive. I put her through a great deal of pain that I might have spared her had I been more caring and compassionate.

There were also times when Mom inadvertently put pressure on my emotional soft spots. She was a perfectionist. I still recall how she asked me to set the table one day—and then went behind me and readjusted what I'd done. I was prone to feeling inadequate already, and this roughed up that emotional wound. Years later Mom told me she'd always loved me more than life itself and regretted that she failed to communicate that in a way that bolstered my self-esteem.

Causing pain isn't limited to family members. I've unwittingly put painful pressure on friends' emotional wounds by failing to use gentleness. This can happen with small issues. For instance, I have a friend who drinks copious amounts of soda. She zealously collects all the cans, and when the piles are high enough, takes them in and recycles them for cash. One day I ribbed her about the practice and suggested perhaps she should just dump the cans in her outdoor bin and let the folks who make their living scavenging for recyclables fish them out and get the money.

My friend felt my comment implied she was being selfish and taking money away from those who needed it more. She let me know that was not the case at all. Her family was going through some rough economic times, and most of the money they had went to meet the needs of her children. But the money from the recycled soda cans represented a tiny bit of freedom she had to do something special for herself now and then—like taking in a movie or buying a small treat. And at times the soda can money was used for necessities. Once the soda can cash filled the gas tank on their car so she could drive her children to school.

I didn't mean to be insensitive, and my teasing was inappropriate. I had inadvertently rubbed salt in her financial wound. I quickly asked her forgiveness.

Being sensitive and gentle with others is so important, be they pets or people. We see this in Jesus' great care and compassion, even when He was dealing with people and their sin.

In John 8 we read the story of a woman caught in adultery. The Pharisees asked Jesus if she should be stoned to death. They knew either a yes or a no could be used to trip up Jesus, and they didn't care how they hurt and humiliated the woman as long as they attained their objective. Jesus' great wisdom and insight thwarted their scheme. He answered, "If any one of you is without sin, let him be the first to throw a stone at her" (John 8:7). After her accusers slunk away, Jesus dealt with the woman. His gentle treatment of her was in stark contrast to the harsh and heartless behavior of the established religious leaders of the time. Jesus simply asked if anyone had condemned her. She said no, and Jesus said, "Then neither do I condemn you…Go now and leave your life of sin" (John 8:11).

Jesus never caused needless hurt. He always used great care in how He dealt with the pain of the people around Him. I'm not perfect as He is, but I have His Spirit within me. If I'm willing to take a little extra time and ask God to guide me, He will show me how to handle others with His gentleness and love.

As God's chosen people, holy and dearly loved, clothe yourselves with compassion, kindness, humility, gentleness and patience (Colossians 3:12).

Consider This

Is there someone in your life you need to handle with special care? How is he or she wounded? How might you be more tender and gentle with your friend or family member?

Is there an area where you've caused needless pain and need to ask forgiveness? Why not take care of it today?

Mario and the Rabbits
God Delivers Us from Our Fears

*If you are distressed by anything external, the pain is
not due to the thing itself, but to your estimate of it;
and this you have the power to revoke at any moment.*

MARCUS AURELIUS

Among many other chores in a farmer's world, there usually comes
a time when something needs to be burned. Almond brush—twigs,
leaves, branches, and old almond pieces left after the harvest—is
a good reason to hold a burn day.

In order to burn anything in our part of the country, we have
to fill out papers and get permission from the appropriate authori-
ties. Greg had done all of that. He'd gotten his fire going and left
two of his employees, Manuel and Hallelujah, to tend it. Some-
time later, he put his two dogs, Meg and Mario, into his truck
and returned to the burn site. The fire had been burning for so
long that part of the mountain of brush had been reduced to a
large pile of ashes. It was a cold day, and with the hot fire, everyone was relaxed.

Greg let the dogs out of the pickup. As was their style, they
romped through the almond orchard, barking and chasing whatever

they could find. As luck would have it, a cottontail rabbit emerged from a hole in the ground. Meg and Mario took off, chasing it around the orchard. Then the rabbit ran into the searing ashes. No one had time to intervene—it just raced in and disappeared.

Meg saw the danger of the fire and was able to pull herself back after barely stepping into its heat. Mario, younger and perhaps not as smart, ran in after the rabbit. After he'd gone about 50 feet into the burning mass, he finally realized his danger. Greg was too far away to reach him, but one of the other guys was closer. He stepped into the red hot ashes, grabbed Mario's collar, and hauled him out.

Both dogs were burned. Meg's feet were somewhat singed, but the pads on Mario's feet were burned off. All the soft skin under his belly was burned too. Greg put the dogs back into the truck and drove them to the vet. She cleaned them up, gave them painkillers and antibiotics, and let Greg take them home to recuperate.

Debbie, Greg's wife, faithfully gave the dogs their medicine. But Greg and Debbie became concerned when all the dogs did was sleep. Mario wouldn't even get up to eat. They checked the medicine bottles and realized they'd misread one of them. It said to give one pill a day, and they'd been giving more. So, as Greg tells it, the dogs were a bit "stoned" on the extra meds. Fortunately, they didn't suffer any worse effects from the error. When the dogs got the proper dosage, they regained their energy, their bodies healed, and they were as good as new.

Though the dogs were back to normal physically, Greg wondered what emotional effects Mario's close call might have on him. Greg found out when he took Mario to work with him again. Where they were going also had a brush fire going. Mario froze immediately when he saw it. Then, as nature would have it, another cottontail ran right in front of him. Mario sprang to life...

and ran under Greg's pickup to hide. Not only did Mario fear fire, but he had a skewed fear of little cottontails!

Have you been afraid of something based on a traumatic experience? My mom had a fear too. She was afraid of water. Her phobia stemmed from her childhood. She was swimming in a pond by her home with other family members and friends. One of her older brothers came to tease her, like big brothers do. He swam up to her, grabbed her, and held her body under the water. He did it once, and when she rose to the surface she yelled for him to stop. He laughed and did it again. This time he held her under a bit too long. She thought she was drowning. Though she'd been a good swimmer before this, she never went swimming again. My whole life I can remember seeing her in a swimsuit, but I never saw her in a pool. She would go with my husband on our boat, but it took a lot of courage. She only did it because she loved him so much.

Mario's skewed fear robbed him of the normal doggie pleasure of chasing rabbits. Mom's fear robbed her of fun in the water. Almost all of us have some kind of fear that limits us and gets in our way. But our God is willing and able to deliver us from our fears if we will turn them over to Him and trust Him.

The Israelites didn't do this though. God told them to go in and conquer the land of Canaan. Moses sent out 12 spies to scout the land, and when they returned, 10 of them said it would be too hard to win battles because the inhabitants were giants. The people chose to believe the majority instead of relying on God, who told them to go in. Instead of entering the Promised Land, the Israelites ended up wandering in the wilderness until a new generation took God at His word and took the land (Numbers 13–14).

Centuries later, another giant, a Philistine named Goliath, dared the armies of Israel to send a champion to fight him. They were horribly frightened, but a shepherd boy named David wasn't. He chose to trust God and fight Goliath for God's glory. David felled Goliath with a slingshot and a single stone. The shepherd boy eventually became a mighty warrior and king. When he faced other trials and was afraid for his life, he wrote, "I sought the LORD, and he answered me; he delivered me from all my fears" (Psalm 34:4).

God is waiting to deliver you too—if you're willing to step out in faith and obedience to Him. Though it may not be easy and the process may take time, He will work with you to get you through it. So when fear starts chasing you, seek the Lord and run into His arms!

When I am afraid, I will trust in you. In God, whose word I praise, in God I trust; I will not be afraid. What can mortal man do to me? (Psalm 56:3-4).

Consider This

Do you have a deep fear of the "rabbit" or "giant" variety? What triggered this fear? How has it gotten in your way? Have you turned it over to the Lord? If yes, how is He helping you work through it? If not, why not talk to Him about it right now?

Blind Fear
God Sees in the Dark

Fear makes the wolf bigger than he is.

GERMAN PROVERB

Mary decided to raise a beautiful Labrador retriever named Zephyr for Guide Dogs of America. This was a big commitment—taking a spirited three-month-old pup and preparing him for a lifetime of service. Zephyr would someday be the eyes and often a decision-making companion of a sight-impaired person.

After having Zephyr for a while, Mary was asked by a friend to bring the puppy to an elementary school to visit a special education class for the seeing impaired. All the children had partial sight except for two, who were totally blind. It was with one of these kids that Zephyr made the closest connection.

The main task of preparing puppies for possible service as guide dogs is socializing them. They must learn to behave well in a variety of situations—from sitting in restaurants to walking through crowds, from being on crowded buses to visiting a school full of children. Zephyr had learned his lessons well. Instead of charging in, tugging at the leash, and barking, he walked into the classroom calmly, with purpose, staying by Mary's side and sitting immediately when she gave the command. One by one each student came up, sat next to Zephyr, and rubbed his belly in exchange for puppy kisses.

As the kids were enjoying their canine visitor, Mary noticed one little girl cowering in the corner. The teacher told her that Stacey had been blind since birth and was deathly afraid of dogs—a fear she'd learned from her mother, who made sure Stacey wasn't ever in the presence of a real dog. No amount of coaxing that day would get Stacey to come anywhere near the "beast."

Over the next few weeks, Zephyr and Mary visited the classroom often. Mary asked Stacey why she was so afraid of dogs. Though Stacey hadn't ever met a dog, she'd heard them bark, and it frightened her. She imagined them to be savage monsters. Though she was blind, Stacey could draw things she'd touched. Mary asked Stacey to draw a picture of what she imagined Zephyr to look like. She drew an imaginary dog whose most prominent feature was big, sharp teeth.

Mary assured Stacey that Zephyr was no kid-eating canine ogre, but a gentle, loving friend. Finally Stacey reluctantly let Mary take her hand and gently stroke it over Zephyr's coat. Zephyr remained amazingly calm—to Stacey's relief. In the days and weeks that followed, Mary patiently guided Stacey's hand over Zephyr's entire body—his tail, legs and paws, even his face—until the fearsome monster in Stacey's mind faded away and was replaced by the reality of a good and gentle puppy. Stacey began to look forward to playing with Zephyr, throwing her arms around him, giggling as he licked her back. Child and dog developed a special bond. When it came time for the visits to end, Stacey told Mary that she was going to do whatever it took so that someday she could have a guide dog just like Zephyr.

When I was a little kid, I was also afraid of what I couldn't see. I was scared of the dark and always made sure my mom left the light on in my room at night. My younger brother and I were sure that a bogeyman lurked in the shadows. All that kept him at bay was that 15-watt light bulb in the Mickey Mouse lamp on the nightstand.

Now it seems silly to be afraid of things that go bump in the night. But before I get too smug, I'm reminded that I am far from being a fear-free adult. The old bogeyman I feared has been replaced by a new one. I even have a name for it: *the future.* I get paralyzed when I think of a future I can't see. I also get nervous when I have to give lectures. Standing all alone in front of a cavernous room full of people and having to talk intelligently for 90 minutes scares me. *What if I freeze up, stammer like a fool, and end up rushing out of the room in disgrace? Or, worse yet, what if I'm boring?*

I was fearful when I had to drop my three-year-old off on his first day of preschool. *What if he hates me for leaving him and has abandonment issues for life?* I worried. And fear crept up my spine when I discovered I had (yet again) left my house keys in the front door overnight. *What if I have Alzheimer's? What if someone saw the keys and came in?*

All of us experience the fear of the big "what if?" Our imaginations conjure up worst-case scenarios of what may or may not happen. Often our fears don't come true. The time we spent in worry and terror turns out to be a complete waste of time and energy.

Whether our fears are well-founded or not, wouldn't it be nice if we had someone or something to help us through them—like Mary helped Stacey? Wouldn't it be nice if we could shine a permanent "night light" on our bogeymen and make them harmless in our minds? Wouldn't it be nice if we had someone who could "see in the dark" and walk alongside us to remind us everything is okay?

Jesus said, "I am the light of the world. Whoever follows me will never walk in darkness, but will have the light of life" (John 8:12). God's Son loved us enough to die for us. He knows the number of hairs on our heads. He knows what we're going to say even before the words form on our lips. He knows our past and present and future. He promises to walk beside us—if we ask Him.

If we let Him be our guide, if we put our fears in the hands of the One who can see in the dark, life will be a lot less scary!

There is no fear in love. But perfect love drives out fear (1 John 4:18).

Consider This

What are your greatest fears? Why? If you trusted God to lead you through them, what difference do you think that would make? What would your life look like?

Old Names or New?

What Do You Answer To?

Words have meaning and names have power.

AUTHOR UNKNOWN

When Mom died and her little Pomeranian, Bebe, came to live with me, I decided to give her a new name. There was nothing wrong with her old one. It just wasn't what I would have chosen. I'd always been fond of the name Becca, so I settled on that. My next task was to teach Bebe that she had a new name.

I started calling my new little dog Becca consistently. I praised and cuddled her when she came to her new name. She learned quickly. But when I tested her, I discovered she came to her old name too. Even months later, when the name "Becca" was firmly etched in her mind, she had a lingering recollection of "Bebe" and responded to it.

Becca isn't the only one in our family who changed names when she changed "parents." Mom lost her birth mother at the age of two. Grandpa remarried not long after. Mom's stepmother changed Mom's name from Yetta to Ethel. Mom was too young to remember, but a relative probably told her about the change.

Decades later Mom told me. What she may not have known was that Yetta was short for something else. After Mom's death a cousin was delving into the family tree and discovered that my mother's given name was really Henrietta.

I was waxing nostalgic one day, so I decided I would dig a little deeper. I looked up "Henrietta" and "Ethel" in a name book. Henrietta meant "home ruler." I had to laugh at that one. A dear family friend once told me my mom liked to rule. Mom's home was her kingdom, and she was most definitely in charge, even in later years when she was frail and in failing health. Ethel meant "noble." That fit too. Mom felt a calling on her life to make a positive difference in the world. In particular, she became deeply and passionately involved in promoting world peace and the rights of nonsmokers. She nobly gave of herself and her resources in these causes until her death.

Mom's names fitting her so well was accidental. Her mom and stepmom didn't pick them on the basis of Mom's personality or characteristics. I didn't pick my dog's name that way either. But when God calls us to leave our old lives and our old master, Satan, and become His children through faith in Christ, He gives us new names He's chosen to fit our new nature.

God's Word says we are children of light, children of God, coheirs with Christ, saints (holy ones), and friends of God. These names encourage us to live lives dedicated to holiness, righteousness, goodness, and truth. God's Word also lets us know that this will be impossible in our own strength. We're reassured that God will help us though: "It is God who works in you to will and to act according to his good purpose" (Philippians 2:13).

Like Becca, I've learned my new names. But also like my dog, I respond to my old ones at times. For instance, I come from a family of high achievers. Though my parents warned me not to,

I judged my worth by worldly standards of success. In my school days, I "succeeded" by getting top grades. When I became a writer, I "succeeded" by earning kudos in my chosen career. If I fell short of my goals, I went into an emotional tailspin and stuck negative labels on myself.

Recently when I received some rewrite suggestions from my coauthors, I reacted negatively. I told myself I was a lousy writer and called myself by old names such as "failure" and "worthless." I was tempted to "come" to the old names that represented that old mindset, but God's Spirit was calling me too. He reminded me I was God's precious child. He brought to my mind that He'd put our writing team together so we could inspire each other to do our best work. With God's help, I ignored the old names and responded only to my new names. I took my coauthors' advice and watched the Lord use it to hone and polish my stories.

We all hear our "old names" at times, and usually more loudly in some situations than others. Becca illustrated this to me. After she became mine, I took her along on some trips back to Mom's house on estate business. In her old environment, Becca reverted to "old name" behaviors, such as wanting to sleep in the kitchen instead of with me and my other dogs on my bed. It reminded me of when I was young in my faith. I'd slip into negative "old name" habit patterns when I went home to see my parents.

One dog trainer recommends giving a rescue dog or a dog new to a family a different name. He says it's part of helping a dog start over in its new life and environment. It encourages the dog to have new associations and move forward. And if the pup was rescued from an abusive situation where it was constantly told "Bad Bruno," it might think it's in trouble when it hears its old name. A new name won't carry that negative load.

I've had Becca just over a year now. As I've been writing this story, she's been sleeping in a dog bed in my office. Just now I tried an experiment. I called her by her old name—Bebe. She looked at me but didn't move. Then I called "Becca." She instantly climbed out of her bed and came to me.

When Becca comes to the name I gave her, it shows others she belongs to me. When we refuse to respond to our old names and live according to our new names in Christ, the world sees we belong to God. So let's answer to our new names and glorify Him!

When your words came, I ate them; they were my joy and my heart's delight, for I bear your name, O LORD God Almighty (Jeremiah 15:16).

Consider This

What are some ways God is calling you to live out your new names in Christ? What are some ways you're tempted to respond to your old names? What is your favorite name from the Lord today? Why?

Patient Beware

Who's Your Spiritual Doctor?

*Physicians and politicians resemble one
another in this respect, that some defend
the Constitution and others destroy it.*

AUTHOR UNKNOWN

Stuart is a Pembroke Welsh corgi—Queen Elizabeth of England's breed of choice. Now that Stuart is past puppyhood, he is sweet and calm and a great lap dog. He loves to sit nearby when I write. He adores lying on the floor near my husband to watch television and nap. Stuart also enjoys playing outside. Most of the time, he's healthy and happy.

One day Stuart developed a medical problem that gave us pause for a while. His first symptoms came without warning. He lay on the floor and began to move his legs as if he were running. Then other uncontrolled movements occurred, lasting for about a minute. Afterward he went outside and ran around for a while in a disoriented manner. Then he came back in and fell sound asleep.

We thought he'd had a seizure. We took him to the vet as soon as we could, but the vet said he didn't know what was wrong. He said we could live with the problem or take our dog to Los Angeles or San Francisco for tests. He didn't know what else to do.

It was time to choose another doctor.

We asked other pet lovers, prayed, and found a wonderful, caring veterinary clinic we now think is the best in town. They did several tests on Stuart. They determined that he had epilepsy, a health problem common in corgis. Thanks to the right diagnosis and care, Stuart's disease is under control except for an occasional seizure. He's living a healthy, happy life.

Unfortunately Stuart isn't the only one in our family who's had medical problems. Some years ago, on the Saturday night before Mother's Day, I got one of those calls no one wants to receive. It was from our son, John. He said, "Mom, I'm on my way to the hospital in an ambulance." He told me he'd been in a motorcycle accident. I took a deep breath and asked, "Are you hurt?" *Duh! He was in an ambulance!* But he replied, "No, I don't think so. Nothing is broken. But I need you to come and get me."

Well, John was wrong. He had a broken leg and broken shoulder. After treating him, the doctor told me to take him home and let him rest. John asked if he needed surgery on his leg, and the doctor said it was up to him. He said John would be able to tell if he needed surgery by how much his leg hurt.

We went home. I suggested John go to my doctor. He refused, deciding he'd wait and see how his leg healed. Almost two weeks later he said, "Mom, my leg isn't getting any better. I can feel the bones moving around in there. Can you get me in to your doctor?" Miraculously, he got an appointment for the next day.

Dr. Coppola looked at John's leg, had X-rays taken, and then sat down beside him. He told John he needed surgery right away. The bones probably weren't going to heal by themselves. He would put a titanium post in John's leg to help strengthen it. Then he asked why we'd waited so long to see him. John reported what the other doctor said. His new doctor sighed, noting that it would have been much better if he'd come in sooner.

After the surgery John healed nicely. He still has some problems, but if we hadn't found the right doctor, the bones in his leg might be rattling to this day.

Just as the right doctors helped John and Stuart get better physically, we all need the right doctor when it comes to our spiritual health. Scripture tells us the Great Physician is our Messiah, Jesus Christ. There are many stories in the Bible that give testimony to His great diagnostic skills and healing power. One of Jesus' apostles, Matthew, wrote:

> Jesus stepped into a boat, crossed over and came to his own town. Some men brought to him a paralytic, lying on a mat. When Jesus saw their faith, he said to the paralytic, "Take heart, son; your sins are forgiven."
>
> At this, some of the teachers of the law said to themselves, "This fellow is blaspheming!"
>
> Knowing their thoughts, Jesus said, "Why do you entertain evil thoughts in your hearts? Which is easier: to say, 'Your sins are forgiven,' or to say, 'Get up and walk'? But so that you may know that the Son of Man has authority on earth to forgive sins…" Then he said to the paralytic, "Get up, take your mat and go home." And the man got up and went home (Matthew 9:1-7).

That man's friends saw only his physical ailment. Jesus, the Great Physician, recognized and diagnosed his spiritual illness as well—and healed both.

Elsewhere in Scripture we're told that Jesus is the only way by which we can come to the Father (John 14:6). He's the only acceptable sacrifice for our sins and the only name under heaven by which our sins can be forgiven (Acts 4:12). But our culture wants us to believe there are many other ways to God. And it is so easy to be misinformed and misdiagnosed by these "false doctors."

Just this week I heard a woman tell some friends that when it came to religion, at least she believed in "something"...and that was all that mattered. But this "something" wasn't Jesus. Though she doesn't realize it, her "false doctor" can't provide an effective diagnosis and treatment for her spiritual ills.

Romans 3:22-24 promises us, "This righteousness from God comes through faith in Jesus Christ to all who believe. There is no difference, for all have sinned and fall short of the glory of God, and are justified freely by his grace through the redemption that came by Christ Jesus."

Have you approached your Great Physician for healing from sin? If not, He is waiting to meet with you right now.

He was pierced for our transgressions, he was crushed for our iniquities; the punishment that brought us peace was upon him, and by his wounds we are healed (Isaiah 53:5).

Consider This

Have you or a loved one gone to see the wrong physical or spiritual doctor? What problems did this cause? Did you find the right doctor? What difference did this make? If you haven't yet come to Jesus for healing from sin, what is stopping you?

The Lesson of the Sausage
Buried Treasure Can't Bless

We make a living by what we get,
we make a life by what we give.

Sir Winston Churchill

Chaz was my cousin Elly's first Hungarian vizsla. He was a handsome hunk of a dog with a close-cropped reddish coat and a lean, muscular, 60-something-pound body. He had a great personality too. He was affectionate and loyal...but also a hoarder.

Elly laughingly recalls that Chaz's goal was to get as many goodies as he could. If someone gave him a treat, he'd take it, go hide it, and come back for another one. When he couldn't get outside to bury his prize, he'd stash it behind a piece of furniture. Over time Chaz could amass a decent amount of "buried" treasure. But his all-time monster haul was what our family calls "The Christmas of the sausage."

In Nebraska, where Elly lived, yards can be blanketed by snow all winter. This particular year was no exception. Chaz's humans were away for the holidays, so a neighbor's son was in charge of feeding and watering the dog. One day when he came to fulfill his dog-care duties, he found a large gift box by the front door. He took it in and left it on the dining room table.

After the boy left, Chaz seized his chance. He knocked that box down and ripped into it. It was filled with candies, cheese, and sausage.

The next day the neighbor found a mess on the floor and cleaned it up, But it was obvious that part of the box's contents was missing.

That March, Elly's yard went through its annual thaw, melting and freezing and melting again until the snow was gone. As this happened, sausages began popping up like spring flowers… except they weren't in very good shape. They were icky and mushy. But Chaz didn't care! He found and ate a bunch before Elly could stop him. The rotten sausages made the dog's stomach roil and produce a lot of gas. Chaz got sick to his tummy more than once. He didn't know the wisdom Jesus shared, "Do not store up for yourselves treasures on earth, where moth and rust destroy, and where thieves break in and steal" (Matthew 6:19). But Chaz reaped the unpleasant results of violating that admonition, and his people suffered with him.

Piling up more than we can use and letting it rot or gather dust or lay buried doesn't help us either. Even if we don't physically sicken, hoarding can rob us and others of the blessings that come from sharing. Cousin Elly applies this principle in an interesting way when it comes to her wardrobe. In January she turns all her clothes hangers with their tops pointing outward. After she wears an item, she reverses the hanger. Next December she can see at a glance which clothes she hasn't put on for a year. She gives all those away.

My parents also believed in sharing their earthly wealth. They chose to live below their means and lend support to organizations that worked to make our world a better place. In her last years, Mom also decided that rather than make her relatives wait for their inheritance, she would give small annual gifts while she was still alive. Instead of "rotten sausage," what popped up for her were love and gratitude and the joy of seeing her gifts change lives. One relative has two beautiful children because she and her husband used Mom's gifts to pay for fertility treatments they couldn't otherwise afford.

After warning that earthly treasures could rot or be snatched away, Jesus urged, "Store up for yourselves treasures in heaven, where moth and rust do not destroy, and where thieves do not break in and steal. For where your treasure is, there your heart will be also" (Matthew 6:20-21).

Why lose your heart to buried treasure? It's far better to share your "sausage" and save your heart for God!

I have seen a grievous evil under the sun: wealth hoarded to the harm of its owner (Ecclesiastes 5:13).

Consider This

Do you have a tendency to "bury sausage"? Why? What is the result? Have you asked the Lord if He wants you to do something else instead? If you've been sharing your "sausage," how has that enriched your life and the lives of others?

Boning Up III
Dogs and Health

1. What is the leading nutritional problem in dogs, and what consequences can it have?

2. What kind of health care might your dog need if it has bad breath?

3. What are some common foods that are fine for humans but toxic for dogs?

4. When can leaving your dog in a parked car be lethal?

5. Is there such a critter as a hypoallergenic dog?

Part 4

Paws for Guidance
Follow Your Alpha

MARTHA & VON

A Teacup in Time
God's Plans Are Best

The best-laid plans of mice and men often go awry.

Robert Burns (ADAPTED)

When my friend Martha was a child she delighted in giving pretend tea parties. She brought out her toy tea set and arranged each place setting with care. She labored over her table, making certain each cup and pot and utensil was arranged just so.

Martha had a boxer puppy named Von. He was a marvelous dog, but he was also full of mischief. He loved to mess up the best-laid plans...er...the tea parties...of little girls. Oftentimes, just when Martha had everything perfect at her tea party, Von would dash up, snatch a teacup in his mouth, and take off.

Naturally Martha was horrified. She didn't go gently into this new game plan! She raced madly after Von, desperate to retrieve her teacup. Von thought the chase was the party. He refused to be easily caught, and many a carefully planned tea party fell by the wayside. So did some of the cups, marked forever by puppy teeth. At the time, little Martha felt frustrated that her puppy had ruined her party.

Half a century later, she views things quite differently.

Chuckling, Martha admitted to me that she couldn't recall a single detail of the childhood tea parties she did manage to give. But she has marvelous memories of her chases through the house after Von. They were Von's way of engaging her, and they helped build a relationship between girl and dog that deeply blessed both their lives. As important as her own agenda seemed at the time, releasing it (however unwillingly) yielded something far better.

And this is even truer when God asks us to release our "best laid plans" and forsake our agenda for His...as I learned in a poignant way two summers ago.

I'd planned what I thought was the perfect people-centered vacation. In early August I'd leave my Los Angeles home and head for Lake Tahoe. I'd spend a day with an out-of-state cousin who planned to be in the area. Then I'd hook up with friends at their family's vacation cabin. We'd drive together to Oregon, and I'd drop them off at their son's home in Bend before motoring on to visit old friends in Portland. While I was gone, a pal who loved animals would pet sit for me.

My table was set and the tea party was about to start. Then my mom tried to steal a teacup. She'd been in ill health for years. Some months earlier she'd suffered a severe heart attack, but now she was recovering reasonably well. She had round-the-clock care at her Santa Barbara home. As my vacation drew near, she felt shaky again. She didn't seem keen on my leaving, and she wanted my help at times that would conflict with my travel schedule.

I felt guilty about leaving Mom, but I was having a really tough time letting go of my much-anticipated "tea party." I wrestled with the matter, but got no peace. Then one day as I was praying, God spoke to me. He let me know He didn't want me that far away from Mom. Then He reminded me I'd always wanted to visit Cambria. This lovely seaside town and artists' colony was just a couple of hours away from Mom's. I could spend part of my vacation with her and the other part on a little Cambria retreat with Jesus. I stopped trying to hang on to my teacup and said yes to God's plan. And God blessed me.

My first four days were spent with Mom. Then I drove to Cambria where God provided a private vacation rental I had all to myself. I had a marvelous time exploring the town. I prowled the shops, took walks by the water, checked out the work of local artists, and even went on a tour at nearby Hearst Castle. I met Christians who prayed for me, and made friends with a local jewelry designer who gave me a showing in her home so I could do early Christmas shopping.

But the most remarkable part of that trip was what God did my very first vacation morning. As I sat over my morning cup of coffee, I was randomly reading through the book of Psalms. A verse stood out—Psalm 68:19: "Praise be to the Lord, to God our Savior, who daily bears our burdens." I felt the Lord was making this promise specifically to me. I assumed that the "burden" was Mom's illness.

But it was much more.

I left Cambria and drove back to Mom's on a Friday afternoon. I planned to return to Los Angeles Sunday after breakfast. At one o'clock on Sunday morning Mom went into acute congestive heart failure. It was the first of many episodes over the following days. She was put on hospice care, and less than three weeks after God gave me that promise in Cambria, Mom passed away.

I'm so grateful God traded my teacup for His agenda. He knew my chances to spend time with Mom were dwindling. He knew if I blew the opportunity, I'd be consumed with guilt later. He knew that instead of long hours driving many hundreds of miles,

I needed time to rest and gather strength for the stresses ahead. And He knew that His promise wasn't just for Mom's illness, but for her death, and for myriad new challenges and responsibilities I would encounter. Even today, over a year later, I'm still peeling back the layers of that promise. I think I will be my whole life.

Decades ago, when I was reeling from a different kind of "stolen teacup," a Christian friend shared some lines from a poem with me. The poem is by Edith Lillian Young and it's called "Disappointment—His Appointment." Perhaps the title says it all. By switching one letter we switch perspective and realize that the thwarting of our plans may make way for God's far better, far wiser purposes for our lives.

Von engaged Martha in a haphazard, self-serving puppy way. God engages us for our greatest good and blessing. So seek God and His will. Trust Him!

In his heart a man plans his course, but the LORD determines his steps (Proverbs 16:9).

Consider This

Has it ever seemed like God was "snatching away your teacup"? How did you feel? What did you do? What was the result? If you had it to do over, would you make a different choice?

The Importance of Traction
Stay on the Best Path

*He makes my feet like the feet of a deer; he
enables me to stand on the heights.*

Psalm 18:33

Shelly came home from a recent trip to find her Wheaten terrier,
MacKenzie, in a bad way. The neighbor who'd been watching the
dog said she'd been falling down a lot. A trip to the vet brought
bad news. Sixteen-year-old MacKenzie's spinal cord was disinte-
grating from old age. Messages between her brain and back legs
were full of glitches, and over time, as the spinal cord continued
to collapse, the damage would progress up her body. For now,
though, everything but her back legs worked fine. Her spirit was
that of a puppy. Because the problem was neurological, she was
in no pain. She just fell a lot, which was confusing and frustrat-
ing for her.

Slippery surfaces, such as Shelly's hardwood and tile floors,
were minefields for MacKenzie. Normal things like walking to
the doggie door and standing at her water bowl eventually became
difficult, if not impossible. Caring friends told Shelly it was time
to put the dog down.

But Shelly loved MacKenzie and refused to give up without a fight. She reasoned, *If a creature is slipping a lot, what does she need? Traction.* So she started adding traction to MacKenzie's world. She went online and ordered four different types of dog shoes. She also bought industrial-sized mud mats to create paths through her house. Where the mud mats were too wide, Shelly bought rubber-backed bathroom throw rugs. The problem with this plan was MacKenzie dragged her rear feet, which would catch the edges of the rugs. The rug would bunch up and trip her. But she always scrambled to get up, usually needing her master's help. MacKenzie wasn't giving up and neither was Shelly.

One day Shelly called, all excited. A new idea was working! Yoga mats. It turns out yoga mats are designed to give traction on both sides. Soon the motley, inefficient rug system was gone and MacKenzie was navigating the house with confidence on a 24-inch-wide pathway of end-to-end cushy yoga mats. She was back in business!

Shelly has turned this into an online business, selling long rolls of yoga mat material to help other owners of aging dogs. She calls them Dogamats, but half of her customers are senior people who also have trouble with slippery floors.

MacKenzie still falls occasionally, but usually it's because she's mistakenly put a paw on the hardwood floor where there's no traction. Her foot will start slipping, which throws her balance off, and down she goes. MacKenzie's solution is to keep her gaze glued to her path. If she comes upon a gap between the mats, where maybe an inch of wood floor is exposed, she'll pause and carefully high-step over the little hazard. The dog understands that the mat means safety. Even a little step off the mat means danger.

MacKenzie could be a role model for all of us! In Hebrews 12, Paul urges us to run the course set out for us, keeping our eyes fixed on Jesus, the author of our faith. (I love that: Jesus wrote my faith.) How many times have I taken my eyes off Jesus, and the next thing I know, I've lost traction. I'm slipping, sliding, and flailing.

A few months ago I read an associate's screenplay and emailed him a critique. I didn't hear back. I emailed again. No reply. I thought we were on good terms and couldn't understand why he wasn't answering. I worried I'd been too harsh and wondered if he hated me now.

I resisted sending more emails. Over the next couple of months condemning thoughts of that critique crept into my mind and distracted me from what I was doing. Then I read that this person had won a writing award. My imagination revved into high gear. I began to wonder if he was emailing peers, telling them what a jerk I'd been with my terribly off-base critique.

As these thoughts were bombarding me, I eventually realized they were the "flaming arrows of the evil one" mentioned in Ephesians 6. The devil was shooting these thoughts into my head to pull my attention away from where God tells me to keep it!

How quickly a good day can turn into doom, gloom, second-guessing, and depression—all because I didn't recognize that the voice I was hearing was the devil's. And then I believed the serpent! That's the misstep…the step off the mat path. One step. One flaming thought to distract me and suddenly I'm MacKenzie stepping off her master's path. Slipping…falling…flailing.

Flailing is an involuntary indicator of desperation. When MacKenzie slips, she flails as she fights to get all four paws back on her rubber path so she has something to dig into. But then she does one other thing, and that makes all the difference. She barks for help. Shelly always comes to her dog's rescue! She puts MacKenzie back on the rubber path, and even supports her until she gets her footing.

In my situation, I was seeing my career tank because I'd given a colleague's script a two-star review. I was flailing. I called out to my Master for help...and He came and provided safe mats. Do you want to know where He put me? Where His path is? Where the traction is? It's in His Word! I called out to God, and in almost no time 2 Corinthians 10:5 came into my head: "We take captive every thought to make it obedient to Christ."

That's what all those flaming arrows were: thoughts. God's Word says to take them captive, to make them obey Jesus Christ. I got traction again. Safety came. I did what the Word said. When one of those fiery darts came at me, trying to make me slip, I followed Jesus' example. When tempted by the devil in the wilderness, Jesus quoted Scripture. So I called on Scripture and locked my attention on what I knew to be true. I refused any thought that I wasn't sure was true. I had no way of knowing what the other writer was thinking or doing, so I stopped entertaining those negative possibilities.

Since I knew my colleague had received an award, I sent a congratulatory note. A few days later, he responded. He was kind and gracious, explaining some of the ways I'd helped him! What a revelation!

When I keep my gaze fixed on Jesus, on what He says is true, I'm safe and moving forward. But if I drop my guard for a second, the devil—who is watching and waiting—is right there to take advantage by trying to distract me. Usually he works with nothing more than a thought. But if I glance at that thought, if I give it a second of my attention, I've taken my gaze off where God told me to keep it. My focus has shifted away from the safety mat. Immediately I'm slipping. I'm down. I'm tangled up in things that aren't even there. I'm being held back, hindered, delayed, hurt, even crushed by imaginary things.

Yes, life is all about traction. That 16-year-old crippled dog has this figured out. Me? I'm still learning.

The LORD will guide you always; he will satisfy your needs (Isaiah 58:11).

Consider This

What are you anxious about? Are you sure it's true? If it's not, how has this lie or half-truth made you lose traction in your walk with God? How can you get your paws back on God's mat?

I'll Take Door Number One

God Shows Us the Way

*The doors we open and close each day
decide the lives we live.*

FLORA WHITTEMORE

Hangover is a beautiful miniature schnauzer named after a bad haircut. When he came to live with my son John, his wife, Sari, and their daughter, Sierra, Hangover changed their lives in bright and exciting ways. They took great care with their new dog by grooming him, training him, and taking him for walks. They also had a doggie door installed so he could go into the backyard whenever he wished. They made sure the yard was enclosed and there was no way he could escape—or so they thought.

One Monday morning after Sierra had gotten on the school bus, she saw Hangover walking down the sidewalk. There was nothing she could do right then, but the minute she got to school, she rushed to the office and called her mom. Sari is a teacher and couldn't leave her students, but she got hold of John, who promised to head straight home from work to corral the truant.

When John got home, he couldn't find Hangover...or his own house key. He'd left it inside. He called his mom (me!) to bring him a spare. I sent it with his sister Karen, who was living with us at the time. Meanwhile, John scoured the neighborhood, but his canine buddy was nowhere in sight. He returned home and found the spot where Hangover had worked a hole in the fence. At this point John felt he really needed to get into the house to see if Hangover had come back, so he bent down and tried to squeeze through the doggie door.

John is not a small person. And he's not "squishy" like me because he works out. But he tried this small door not meant for humans. He shoved his shoulders through, but then he got stuck… halfway in, halfway out. Now he had a new challenge! As hard as he struggled, he couldn't get loose. Finally his head rested on the floor from exhaustion. The noise startled Hangover, who'd been quietly resting inside on the sofa. He jumped down, ran over, and licked John's face. Seeing his dog and being licked all over his face, John relaxed and managed to slide back out the doggie door. Hangover joined him outside, and they waited together for Karen.

Though that dog door was perfect for Hangover, it wasn't designed for John. He got into trouble by trying to go through the wrong door. Spiritually speaking, the same thing can happen to us when we're seeking God's presence. Today's culture tells us there are many ways or "doors" to God, but Scripture tells us there is only one. Jesus said, "I am the way and the truth and the life. No one comes to the Father except through me" (John 14:6).

I had a friend in college who wanted desperately to find God, but she kept getting stuck in the wrong doors. One of her professors told her there were many ways to God. He suggested she try to go through the portals of chanting and meditation. I shared John 14:6 with her, and also John 10:9: "I [Jesus] am the gate; whoever enters through me will be saved. He will come in and go out, and find pasture."

My friend couldn't make up her mind to try this door. She felt confused and lost. She sat next to me during many lunches and asked questions. I tried to help her understand that Christ is *the* door to God. But her professor was telling her about other doors, and she felt she needed to try them.

John got worn out when he tried the wrong door, but he backed up and entered his house through the door meant for him once Karen brought him the key. When my friend tried the wrong doors, she stayed stuck. Sadly, she hasn't yet pulled herself loose from those doors of chanting, meditation, and the influence of her professor. She didn't try to enter God's presence through the only door big enough to let her in—Jesus.

None of us can walk through God's door unless His Spirit enables us. None of us can pry people loose from the wrong doors. But we can pray for God's Spirit to do this. I pray that one day my friend will get unstuck and walk through God's door and into the newness of life in Christ.

Jesus said again, "I tell you the truth, I am the gate for the sheep" (John 10:7).

Consider This

Have you ever been stuck in the wrong spiritual door? What lured you there? What kept you from pulling free? How did God's Spirit pry you loose?

Unexpected Blessings
God Gives Good Gifts

God's gifts put man's best dreams to shame.

ELIZABETH BARRETT BROWNING

On that day in the early 1990s, as Pastor Andy drove a group of teens home from a mission trip to help flood victims in Kansas, the last thing on his mind was an unexpected blessing from God. Then he spotted some movement by the side of the road. When he pulled over to investigate, he found five whimpering German shepherd/Lab puppies huddled in a ditch.

Andy knew he couldn't leave them there. But he and his wife, Mary, didn't want the responsibility of one dog right now, much less five puppies. They were already super-busy with church and had two energetic little girls, ages two and four. But what could he do? He loaded the five little pups into his car, fully intending to nurse them back to health and then give them to nice homes.

As soon as Andy's four-year-old daughter Hannah saw the pups, she cried out that God had answered her prayers! She'd been asking God for a dog every night for the past year. Though her parents had repeatedly told her the timing wasn't right, she and her little sister kept praying, undeterred by the wisdom of their parents.

Andy and Mary eventually relented and decided to keep one puppy. They named her Chum. Fears that a dog would be too much for the family proved groundless. Chum was a great and loyal pet for 13 years. The whole family acknowledged her as a special, handpicked gift from God.

God has also given me blessings that weren't quite what I had in mind. When I started shopping for a house, I was a single guy with a freelance writing career. I was doing reasonably well, but even so there was no guarantee my income would be steady. I calculated how much money I'd have if I were collecting unemployment and renting a room. Based on those figures, I set a firm upper-price limit on what I could afford.

I looked at what seemed like hundreds of houses. I made offers but was turned down. Finally I found a place that felt right. I'd heard that the top three considerations in buying a home are location, location, and location. I prayed about it. This location was right. It felt like home. The only problem was that its cost exceeded my price limit. What's more, it had only been on the market a couple of days and there were three other interested parties. The real estate agent told me I'd have to "up" my bid *now* if I wanted this place.

After I hung up the phone, I prayed: "Please, Lord, speak to me in an 'audible' voice, like the donkey spoke to Balaam. Is this house a gift from You or a money-pit from the devil?"

I didn't hear an audible voice, but a Scripture came to mind: "My God will meet all your needs according to his glorious riches in Christ Jesus" (Philippians 4:19). Was that enough to bank on?

I guess it was. The next thing I knew I was calling the Realtor back and giving her the go-ahead to raise my bid. She told me I'd made the right decision, and we'd know the outcome first thing in the morning. I tossed and turned all night, struggling with a major bout of buyer's remorse. Was I insane? Why did I want a house? I wasn't married. I didn't have a family. Those things weren't even a blip on my bachelor radar. I had money in the bank and was living an easy life. By renting a penthouse in downtown Los Angeles I had no upkeep. I could lock the door and go on worry-free vacations. I didn't even have to strain my arm to enter the building—there was a doorman.

Buying a house would deplete my savings. Its yard would need to be cared for. Since it had been built in 1951, this house would eventually need new plumbing, new electrical, and a new roof. And what if there was an earthquake?

I began to hope I'd lose the bidding war, that I'd get a conciliatory call in the morning from the agent saying better luck next time. I'd pretend to be sad about the loss. Then, as soon as she hung up, I'd heave a sigh of relief.

But when morning came, my agent congratulated me. I was a new homeowner! That was 16 years ago. Even though I paid more than I wanted and deal with the ups and downs of freelance work, I've never missed a mortgage payment. I've managed to replace the plumbing and the roof, and we're currently doing a major remodel. And, like Andy and Mary and their girls looking back on their 13 God-blessed years with Chum, I look back and marvel about how this house has been a blessing for me.

Because God gave me a house, I wound up getting a dog— one I couldn't have in that luxury condo. Gracie changed my life and taught me great and unsearchable truths I didn't know (see our first book for dog lovers called *Four Paws from Heaven*). Late one night when Gracie cajoled me into taking her out for a walk, I witnessed a hit-and-run accident involving my neighbors' car. Up until then these neighbors had been strangers. Now we got acquainted. Next thing I knew, they invited me to a local church where I met my future wife.

We started married life in this house, and a few years later our son, Skye, was born. When he reached school age, we discovered our home is in an excellent school district. That meant we didn't have to send him to a costly private school. And because we have a child in school, we're meeting other neighbors who have kids in school—a "species" that was nonexistent to me in my single guy world.

Thanks be to God who knows our hearts, our desires, and our needs. And He delights to bless us in unexpected ways if we trust in Him.

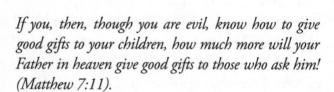

If you, then, though you are evil, know how to give good gifts to your children, how much more will your Father in heaven give good gifts to those who ask him! (Matthew 7:11).

Consider This

What was the best gift someone gave you that you wouldn't have picked for yourself?

What has God given you that you wouldn't have chosen on your own?

Eat the Chicken and Spit Out the Bones

Seek God's Discernment

*We must make the choices that enable us
to fulfill the deepest capacities of our real selves.*

THOMAS MERTON

Several days after a family barbecue, our dog Stuart got sick. Anything he ate or drank came back up. He lost weight and became lethargic. We took him to the vet. They ran tests, took X-rays, and decided Stuart had a blockage in his intestines. They weren't sure if it was food or a tumor. They asked if they could do surgery right away, and we agreed.

When they got inside our dog, the doctors found a one-inch piece of corn cob that Stuart must have gobbled off the ground or stolen off someone's plate. If they hadn't done surgery, our beloved pet would have died. As it was, we brought him home after a few days in the pet hospital, and he recovered nicely. Had he eaten the corn and spit out the cob, he wouldn't have had a problem. We were so pleased God allowed Stuart to spend more time with us!

In a different way than Stuart, I got blocked up too. Years ago

I went back to college. When I was finishing up my degree in philosophy and religious studies, I had to take a course that made me choke. I got terribly upset at all the extras that were added to the class requirements. I had to write papers on topics I totally disagreed with. I had to listen to lectures I felt were a waste of time.

I called a minister friend of mine and told him my problem. He shared some simple, wonderful words I'll never forget. He said I just had to eat the chicken and spit out the bones.

That was the verbal surgery I needed to get unblocked. I'd been feeling trapped. I'd been "under" my circumstances. Now I put myself back under God's protection. Rather than letting my situation control my life, I chose to let God do so.

I took what I needed from the course materials and spat out the rest. I depended on my Savior, and He helped me through. I went on to get my degree and follow God's call to become a schoolteacher.

We all face situations where we need to know chicken from bones and spit out what is getting in our way. The Old Testament prophet Elijah was no exception. God used him mightily in a showdown with the prophets of Baal on Mt. Carmel. They were exposed as phonies, and God's power was revealed. This didn't please Jezebel, the idolatrous wife of Israel's King Ahab. She sent a messenger to tell Elijah she would have him killed.

Elijah choked! He ran for his life. He told God he'd had enough and wanted to die. But God sent an angel with bread and water to strengthen Elijah. The prophet journeyed to Mt. Horeb, and God spoke to him there and asked why he'd come. Elijah told God, "I have been very zealous for the LORD God Almighty. The Israelites have rejected your covenant, broken down your altars, and put your prophets to death with the sword. I am the only one left, and now they are trying to kill me too" (1 Kings 19:14).

Elijah couldn't see the chicken for the bones. He was "under" his circumstances. God responded by performing spiritual surgery. He told Elijah to return and appoint specific men as kings of Aram and Israel. He told Elijah to anoint Elisha to take over as prophet. These men would be instruments of God's judgment. And then God added, "Yet I reserve seven thousand in Israel—all whose knees have not bowed down to Baal and all whose mouths have not kissed him" (verse 18). There were apparently still some "chicken" in Israel, and God pointed this out.

Just like the vets removed the corn cob from Stuart's stomach, God removed Elijah's "bone" and freed the prophet to get back on His game plan. Do you need something removed in your life? If you seek God and submit to His wisdom, He will help you eat the chicken, spit out the bones, and stay under His umbrella.

Give your servant a discerning heart to govern your people and to distinguish between right and wrong. For who is able to govern this great people of yours? (1 Kings 3:9)

Consider This

When were you last in a situation where you needed to "eat the chicken and spit out the bones"? What blocked you up? How did you deal with it?

Luna's Tangled Web

Let God Focus You

*If the heart wanders or is distracted, bring it back
to the point quite gently and replace it tenderly in
its Master's presence. And even if you did nothing
during the whole of your hour but bring your
heart back and place it again in our Lord's presence, though it went away every time you brought
it back, your hour would be very well employed.*

St. Francis de Sales

Luna lives in a nice, clean house with a small manicured yard—a fairly tame environment for a young, energetic dog. So when Chris brings out the leash, meaning *walk,* Luna is 200 percent ready to run. She is filled with curiosity and excitement about the outside world. When the front door opens, it's all Chris can do to hold on to that leash. Once outside, Luna's five senses rev into overdrive. If Luna were a motorboat, Chris would be the water skier. Luna makes a mad dash onto the neighbor's lawn, her nose sniffing out new smells like a prospector mining for gold. Chris tugs her back to the sidewalk, but soon she spots a dropped ice-cream cone. Luna pulls like a tractor to give it a lick. Then she lifts her head, ears perked up. "What's this? Barking around the block? Let's go that way. No, wait! Look! I spy a cat sitting on a fence. Let's chase it!"

All too often Luna winds up completely tangled in her leash, hog-tied like a calf in a rodeo event. Chris has to stop and, as if solving a brain-teasing puzzle, painstakingly "unpretzel" his dog. He gives her a strong admonition to walk only where he, her master, leads. If she continues to disobey, Chris is forced to bring out the choke chain. It's for Luna's own good and safety and will cause no discomfort as long as she behaves herself.

Like Luna, I'm sometimes tempted to strain at my leash and chase a host of distractions. I was born, raised, and still live in Los Angeles county, home to a Hollywood dream factory that exports a smorgasbord of tempting entertainment to the world. As a screenwriter, I'm a tiny cog in that vast and complex machine. Though to the casual observer I may appear to live a nice, clean, manicured life, when I sit down to write a movie my mind races out my front door and into a wild and crazy world where anything is possible.

When I'm raring to go, the last thing I want is to be restrained by my Master tugging at my leash. Though God may want to lead my writing "this way," I may long to yank it "that way." Like a dog wanting to chase a cat or follow the call of a distant bark, I've chased many elusive dreams and followed the siren calls of seductive idols.

Ever since my undergraduate days, I longed to be "successful." Making a modest living writing screenplays and song lyrics wasn't enough. I wanted more. Instead of steadfastly seeking God and meditating on His truth to light my way, I followed the wisdom of this world. I wrote what I thought would sell.

A number of years ago, when horror was hot, I tried to write an R-rated supernatural slasher film. I banged out a first draft in eight weeks. Over the next few years, I rewrote that script to death. I went around and around in circles and had a number of well-meaning friends and producers give me critique notes. I read horror books and scripts and watched horror films. I did everything I could short of selling my soul to make this screenplay work and find a company interested in producing it.

Finally, after 13 drafts, I realized my script was going nowhere. I'd raced down my own paths, fooling myself that I was going God's way. I'd tangled myself in my own creative web. So I had to ask God, in His mercy, to come beside me and lovingly "unpretzel" my leash. That meant letting go of the script—and the hundreds of hours invested in it—and moving on to other projects. Maybe one day God will lead me to rewrite that screenplay...or maybe not. I only know I'm choosing to obey His commands and follow His lead.

I was trying to write a film about the devil and spiritual warfare. Such a task is not to be taken lightly. I think of it as me driving a bus down a steep, rocky path. If I get distracted for even a moment, I may plunge off that path and write a mindless exploitation film that glorifies violence and the dark side. Writers and bus drivers have a great responsibility. If they veer off the road and crash, they take many others with them. Drivers, keep your eyes on the road! Writers, keep your eyes on God and His truths!

One way to keep my eyes on God's truths is to heed the tug of His leash. That leash is His Word. God's Spirit uses the Word to tug on my heart. If I continue to strain against Him, the Spirit convicts my heart of sin, which serves as a choke chain to bring me up short for my good so I'll submit and get back on God's path.

Jesus said, "Whoever serves me must follow me" (John 12:26). If we take time to be still, check our hearts, repent of our sins, and follow God's path, our lives and work will produce good fruit that glorifies our Master.

Trust in the LORD with all your heart and lean not on your own understanding; in all your ways acknowledge him, and he will make your paths straight (Proverbs 3:5-6).

Consider This

What things and people have lured you off God's path? How has that tangled you up? Did you let God "unpretzel" you? How did He do that?

Door or Wall?
Wait for God's Timing

Our patience will achieve more than our force.

EDMUND BURKE

Shelly called Cody, her beloved Wheaten terrier, "The Forrest Gump of Dogs." He was sweet but not the brightest bulb in the pack. His learning curve was a straight line, and experience was not his teacher. Like all dogs, Cody greatly anticipated outings, and he was especially fond of riding in the car. When Shelly jangled her car keys Cody's body launched into high alert. As they walked out to the garage, the sight of Shelly's Ford Explorer drove him into a delirious state of expectancy. All Shelly had to do was reach for the SUV's door latch to trigger Cody's response. He was so anxious to get in that he'd leap before the door was fully open, hit the door, and bounce off, landing on the concrete with a "Duh?" look on his face. And Cody never learned. Unless Shelly restrained him, he would fling himself against that partially open door every time. Because of his impatience and inability to wait on his master, the door to desire became a wall.

My wife and I had a similar experience with respect to desire and cars. When Celine and I married, we had old cars. I owned a 1960 Austin Healey 3000 I only drove to church on Sundays and a 1989 Toyota pickup with a stick shift. Celine brought a 1991 Ford Tempo with peeling paint and an overheating radiator into the marriage. Realizing a reliable vehicle would soon become a necessity, we committed to purchase a new or slightly used car before either of us had a major breakdown on the road.

Hoping for the best with our limited budget, the first "door" we tried to enter was the classified ads. We zeroed in on late model, low mileage cars with prices too good to be true. We discovered the world of reconditioned salvaged vehicles. These were newer cars that were totaled and then bought by mechanics who quick-fixed them for fast sale. These cars may look new, but consumer groups warn that "salvage cars" often have major problems that will surface later. We realized our hours of online research, phone calls, and tracking down leads was all for naught. We'd tried to leap through a semi-closed door and bounced off a wall.

Okay. No more fooling around with used cars. We decided to push our finances and take a leap of faith through the new car door. Our Sunday paper was filled with offers of new cars with prices too good to be true. When we went out to look at our chosen models, we discovered the world of bait and switch. Like an innocent little trout, a buyer bites into what appears to be a two-cent worm—and the next thing he knows he's hooked into paying caviar prices.

When I looked at the full-page ads, I failed to notice the carefully hidden tiny words like "one only." When customers show up at the car lot, this "one only" car is usually sold, and the salespeople take the prospective buyers to look at a "great deal" on a similar car...except it costs $2000 more and comes with a $2000 alarm system the buyers don't want. Or maybe the "one only" car is hot pink. After weeks of repeating variations of these scenarios, Celine and I felt like—hmmm—a frustrated dog flinging himself against the closed door of a Ford Explorer.

We began to rethink the car we wanted. We could settle for a cheaper, less reliable model. We could save money if we didn't get air conditioning or a factory-installed stereo. We considered a car with a manual transmission for $1000 less. I told Celine if the dealer accepted our lowball offer I'd teach her how to shift gears. It wasn't accepted, and I have yet to teach her how to drive a stick. We continued to downgrade our desire, and in moments of weakness considered another foray into the principalities of the previously owned.

For months we flung ourselves at a variety of doors hoping they would lead to the car of our dreams—only to find those doors were actually walls and perhaps this dream car only existed in the garage of our minds. We were as frustrated as a dog yearning for a joyride that can't get into the back of his master's vehicle.

We did pray throughout the duration of our car-shopping crusade. But prayer is one thing, and waiting on God to open the door is quite another.

Then one day we saw an especially low price for our number one model of car. Now educated in the ways of the car world, I called and asked how many of the "three only" vehicles were available. A salesman named Rick said all of them. I asked what color they were. He said one red metallic and two sand metallic—colors we could live with.

I drove to the dealership and met Rick. He showed me the cars. They were just as they were represented in the ad. And the price? Exactly as quoted! I waited for Rick to suddenly recall the $2000 stereo or the $3000 extended warranty that were an inseparable part of the package. But that other shoe didn't drop. Next thing

I knew, I was in the sales office signing papers. As we chatted, I found out Rick was a Christian. And so was the finance guy.

What happened next was surreal—like entering a land where cows fly and dogs talk. All three of us prayed over the contracts and the deal. It was the most amazing retail experience of my life! To this day, Celine and I feel this car was a gift from God. After months of flinging ourselves against walls and hitting the floor with a thud, what a delight to be ushered through an open door!

We invited Rick and his wife to a Christmas party—and they came. The next week, as we were driving to a family event on Christmas Day, we glanced into the next lane and there they were, in the car beside us, waving and wishing us a Merry Christmas.

When we bring our requests to God, waiting on His answer will make all the difference in the world. Why not choose to stop hitting the wall and wait for God to open the door.

When I arrived in Troas to proclaim the Message of the Messiah, I found the place wide open: God had opened the door; all I had to do was walk through it (2 Corinthians 2:12 MSG).

Consider This

Have you tried to walk through a door and hit a wall? When God opens doors, how is that different?

Stuck in the Gulley
Who Is Leading Your Life?

God often takes a course for accomplishing His purposes
directly contrary to what our narrow views
would prescribe. He brings a death upon
our feelings, wishes, and prospects when
He is about to give us the desire of our hearts.

John Newton

Sam, a pastor, was also an avid skier. His dog, Laska, loved to join in the fun. Laska was so eager that if Sam was skiing with friends, the border collie would plunge down the mountain with whoever took off first, whether it was his master or not.

That's how Laska happened to be chasing a snowboarding friend of Sam's down a ridge on Mammoth Mountain in California. Sam wasn't far behind on his skis. Sam's friend sped down the slope until it narrowed to a gulley between outcroppings of rock. There he halted, and Laska stopped too.

Maybe the dog glanced back to see where Sam was. Maybe he just looked up at the sky. For whatever reason, Sam's friend headed down again, and Laska never noticed. Suddenly Laska was in the gulley by himself. He didn't have Sam's friend to follow, and he didn't know which way to go. He looked up the hill at his master and whimpered.

Sam saw how his dog was acting and realized Laska was stuck and scared. He skied down and gently coaxed the dog to follow him to safety.

Laska's dilemma is a great picture of what can happen to us if we get ahead of our Master. Sam could certainly relate because he'd experienced something similar when he was newly married.

The young couple lived in Mammoth Lakes. They longed to spend more time together, but because of their jobs they rarely saw each other. They were in a rough place. Then Sam learned of an opportunity with a wilderness ministry. He and his wife could work together, and they both loved the outdoors. Sam felt called to ministry so the situation seemed perfect.

Well, almost perfect. Deep down, Sam had some nagging doubts. He'd been contemplating going back to school. His dream was to teach theology at a college or become a pastor. He'd sensed for a long time that this was his call from the Lord. Was this new opportunity what God wanted them to do?

Looking back, Sam feels he and his wife didn't think and pray the situation through enough. Rather than make the hard decision to hold out for school, they gave in to the lure of this fun new wilderness job. Sam rationalized his doubts away. He and his wife signed on, pulled up stakes, and moved from the eastern side of the Sierra to the western side.

The young couple's eagerness had them plunging down the mountain ahead of their Master, not fully realizing they were chasing their own agenda rather than God's.

They found out soon enough.

The prerequisite to starting their jobs was a two-week training course offered only once a year. Just before coming, Sam's wife, a runner, had pulled a muscle in a marathon. Her injury acted up, and she was unable to complete the course. Sam got on board with the ministry, but his wife was told she couldn't be hired until she finished the training 12 months later. She was forced to seek other employment.

Suddenly the newlyweds were back to square one, working separate jobs and hardly ever seeing each other. They actually had less time together than ever. Sam realized they couldn't sustain this, but he'd made a long-term commitment to the ministry. He wrestled with the situation, but he felt he shouldn't break his word. He and his wife were stuck in a gulley. They now realized they'd gotten ahead of God.

Like Laska, they looked to their Master for rescue. They prayed to be let out of their commitment, and when they asked, the ministry agreed.

God was leading them out of the gulley! They followed His lead, went back to Mammoth, and got involved in a church plant. Ultimately that resulted in Sam going to seminary. They were back on the Lord's agenda, following His path for them down the mountain of life.

Sam believes the misstep he made stemmed from spiritual immaturity. These days he's more thorough when he seeks God's guidance. He also feels God used the situation to help shape and mold his character. He learned humility, the need to be open, and that sometimes it's best to do the hard thing...admit he'd made a mistake.

Sam also learned another lesson he's found useful. He says churches, officials, and pastors can be tempted to "ski down the mountain ahead of God." They can grab on to techniques or programs that look good to them without really asking God what He wants them to do. There can be an unconscious attitude of

"God, follow me when I do this." The newest program or technique might be great, but it also might not be God's best for the organization or individuals. Much prayer and a sincere seeking to discover where God is working and what He is doing is crucial. The need to identify and join in God's game plan is true whether ministering to a church, a family, or an individual.

Though Laska got ahead of Sam on the mountain, the moment he looked back for help, his loving master was right there to guide him. Our loving Lord is right here to guide us too. He knows us better than we know ourselves, so He will lead us down the paths that will bless us most and serve Him best.

I will instruct you and teach you in the way you should go; I will counsel you and watch over you. Do not be like the horse or the mule, which have no understanding but must be controlled by bit and bridle or they will not come to you (Psalm 32:8-9).

Consider This

Is there a time in your life when you got stuck in a gulley? What caused the problem? How did God lead you out? What did you learn that helps you follow God's leading? How can you share that with others?

Earthquake Sensory Perception
Heed God's Early Warning Signs

*None pities him that is in the snare, who
warned before, would not beware.*

ROBERT HERRICK

Steve was walking in his neighborhood when he came across an injured dog. Wondering if it had been the victim of a hit-and-run driver, Steve was torn about what to do. Should he leave this shaggy mutt in the street or take him home? Steve was single, lived in an apartment, and didn't have time to care for a dog. But heart overruled logic. He took the dog back to his place and made a comfortable spot for it in the kitchen. The dog lay limp, as if its legs could no longer hold the weight of its body. For the next few days the injured animal barely moved. He stayed curled up on the floor.

Then one fateful morning Steve woke up early to check on the injured dog he'd named Rusty. When he opened the kitchen door, Rusty was standing bolt upright. Up till now, the dog hadn't done this, so it was an eerie sight. For a few moments Steve saw Rusty standing perfectly still, as if on high alert. Then the magnitude 6.7 Northridge Earthquake struck. It rocked Steve's apartment building and all of Southern California. When it was over, Steve realized Rusty knew that earthquake was coming before it happened. He was convinced that Rusty was hooked into a source of information outside the realm of a human's five senses.

There is controversy among seismologists about whether dogs can sense earthquakes, with top scientists on both sides of the debate. Those who do believe dogs have "ESP" (earthquake sensory perception) can't explain how dogs know. They are heavily invested in solving this mystery because a reliable early warning system for earthquakes could prevent countless injuries and save many lives.

There are other early warning systems that are also somewhat mysterious. Dreams are one. Years ago I experienced an "early warning" dream. I met someone who appeared to be a nice Christian lady. Looking back, there were warning signs that she wasn't the right person for me, but like the guy in Proverbs 7:22 who "followed [the temptress] like an ox going to the slaughter," I ignored the flashing red lights and raced full speed ahead.

One night I had a very vivid dream—the kind that's so real I wasn't sure it was a dream. My lady friend came over and gave me a hug. Suddenly she morphed into the biggest boa constrictor I'd ever seen. This monster snake wrapped around me and did what boa constrictors do best—constrict. Frozen stiff with whatever emotion goes beyond mind-numbing, bowel-quivering terror, I knew I had to call out to Jesus. But that Name stuck in my gullet like a chicken bone as I struggled to get enough air. Just as I felt I was about to die—I managed to scream out, "Jesus!"

Then I woke up.

I believe that dream was from God. He was warning me that this relationship was an impending disaster. Like someone in a flimsy building during an earthquake, I got out fast!

Yes, God uses dreams as early warning signs. When Abraham was sojourning in a potentially hostile land with his fetchingly beautiful wife, Sarah, he told everyone she was his sister. Abimelech, King of Gerar, was interested in Sarah and sent for her. But before Abimelech could be with Sarah, he was warned by God in a dream: "You are as good as dead because of the woman you have taken; she is a married woman" (Genesis 20:3). Abimelech "ran for safety" by returning Sarah to her husband.

When the Magi told King Herod of their quest to find "the one who has been born king of the Jews," he responded, "As soon as you find [the Christ child], report to me, so that I too may go and worship him" (Matthew 2:8). But if those wise men had any inclination to do so, God quickly put the kibosh on it. In Matthew 2:12 we read, "Having been warned in a dream not to go back to Herod, they returned to their country by another route."

Thank God for His early warning systems. It matters not whether they come through our five senses, other believers, His Spirit, His Word, or through dreams. When God speaks, we need to listen!

If those who ignored earthly warnings didn't get away with it, what will happen to us if we turn our backs on heavenly warnings? (Hebrews 12:25 MSG).

Consider This

Has God ever warned you of an impending disaster? By what means? Did you listen and obey? What was the result?

And God Sent a Dog...

Seek...and God Will Guide You

*We have ample evidence that the Lord
is able to guide. The promises cover every
imaginable situation. All we need to do is to
take the hand he stretches out.*

ELISABETH ELLIOT

Sometimes God uses animals in unusual ways to get our attention. With an Old Testament prophet named Balaam, He used a talking donkey (Numbers 22). With my friend Mark, God used a wise canine.

As a young man, Mark made a commitment to follow Christ. But somewhere along the way he strayed from the righteous path. Although he had a great girlfriend, a nice car, and high hopes of achieving success in the film business, beneath his confident veneer all was not well. He felt spiritually lost. Desperate to reconnect with Jesus, Mark dropped everything and set out on a three-day backpacking and fasting trek in the rugged Sespi Wilderness in California. He took along his handsome and powerful 125-pound St. Bernard/German shepherd mix named Smokey.

After a couple of days of wandering, Mark became utterly lost in the wild country—an ironic metaphor for his spiritual condition.

No matter how much he backtracked and searched, he couldn't find the trail…or Jesus. Waves of panic washed over him. He felt completely immobilized. At his wit's end, and for reasons he can't recall, Mark knelt down and looked into Smokey's eyes. In all seriousness, he asked, "Where's the trail?"

Mark had never talked to Smokey like this and never taught him the meaning of the word "trail," but Smokey instantly dashed off and, in a few bounds, scaled a nearby rugged 15-foot rock wall. Mark quickly scrambled up to join Smokey and found, to his utter shock, that he was back on the trail. Tears filled his eyes as he hugged his dog. How did Smokey understand his cry for help? Mark didn't get an audible answer from Smokey, but as he and his dog walked on, Mark got an answer in his heart. A still, small, inner voice reassured him that Jesus would always be his guide, would always direct his steps, if only he would ask.

I've also experienced the terror of being lost. One of my earliest memories is from first grade. When school was over, I was supposed to walk out front with a friend and wait for his mom to pick us up. On this particular day I got distracted and went to the corner store to check out the candy instead. By the time I got back to the meeting place, no one was there. I couldn't find my friend or his mom. I looked up and down the street for his mom's familiar car, but it was nowhere to be seen. I still remember the rising panic of being lost and alone. I wasn't sure if I could find my way home by myself. I was on the verge of tears, and I must have looked desperate.

An unfamiliar car pulled up and a stranger leaned over and asked if I needed a ride. Today, as the parent of a young child myself, I realize the danger of this. Child abduction is probably in the top three of the all-time greatest parental fears. Children should *never* accept a ride from a total stranger. But that day I climbed into the car and told the man my home address (which I'd dutifully memorized). The man took me home, and I escaped without harm—except for the punishment my very worried-but-thankful mother gave me when she learned what I'd done. Looking back, I believe God kept me safe.

I'm older now, but God still watches over me when I'm lost. A few years ago I was sent to Shanghai to do research for a movie. I'm a fourth-generation Chinese-American with a toddler's command of Mandarin. I was raised on a cultural diet of Western staples such as *Gilligan's Island* and *Mad* magazine. I felt completely lost in this bustling city of more than 20 million people. I stayed in a Chinese-speaking hotel and had only one English-speaking contact, who promptly told me she had to leave the next day on a business trip to Beijing. I was going to be left to fend for myself.

I didn't know how to get around the city. I hadn't figured out the local money. I wasn't even sure how to buy food. Like the lost six-year-old who'd missed his ride home, I felt familiar waves of panic washing over me. *What if I get hit by a car? What if I'm mugged? What if I become deathly ill or am mistakenly arrested? Who can I call?*

Then I remembered to call on God. I got down on my knees and prayed. God answered—not through a talking donkey or a miraculously responsive dog, but by giving me a commonsense idea. I asked my contact if she could give me the phone number of a local, English-speaking person I could call in case of an emergency. She obligingly wrote down the number of a TV commercial producer she'd worked with in the past. Out of all the people she could have chosen, my "randomly selected" new contact turned out to be an on-fire, Spirit-filled, Bible-believing one-man army for Jesus.

"Tony" eventually took me to an incredible church where the message blew me away. I went to his small group and gave testimony about being a believer in Hollywood. I met an amazing network of Chinese Christians in the media. And when Tony came to America shortly thereafter, he stayed at my house. We've been great friends ever since and still pray together on the phone.

When Mark felt lost, God used a dog to help him get back on the right physical trail...and the right spiritual trail as well. When I felt lost as a six-year-old, God used a kind stranger to get me home. And God kept me safe too. When I felt lost in Shanghai, God not only provided an English-speaking contact person, but also a true brother who spoke the same "spiritual language" I did and made my visit to China a spiritual milestone.

I find it reassuring to know that God never forsakes or abandons His children. No matter our ages, Jesus always watches over us. Our Creator is willing and able and incredibly inventive in helping the lost find their way back home...to Him.

I [the LORD] will guide you along the best pathway for your life. I will advise you and watch over you (Psalm 32:8 NLT).

Consider This

What is your most memorable childhood episode of being lost? How did you feel? What did you do? What or who helped you find your way?

Have you ever felt spiritually lost? How did God help you find your way to Him? Do you feel spiritually lost right now? Talk to God and ask Him to help you. He will!

A Shepherd's Heart
Stay on God's Job Site

*Be faithful in small things because it is
in them that your strength lies.*

MOTHER TERESA

Pastor Sam Adams is bi-vocational. His tiny church can't pay much, so he also works full-time in construction. His border collie, Laska, is the perfect "job dog." Border collies are bred to be herders, so Laska's instinct is to watch over his charges and keep them together. In the absence of sheep to care for, Laska views Sam and his fellow workers as his herd.

At least that's Sam's take. When he brings Laska along to a job site, his dog stays right there. Not so a fellow worker's Labrador, who seems born to wander. Laska resists, even when his strong instinct to play dictates otherwise. Once three strange dogs showed up on a site. Laska frolicked and romped with them until the other dogs crossed the street. At that point Laska lay down and watched. He wouldn't follow the other dogs. Only once can Sam remember Laska straying, and that was when he went to play with some children in a nearby field. Sam isn't quite sure what prompted that shift in behavior, but it hasn't recurred.

Laska's herding instinct also comes out with Sam's three small children. When they play, he runs circles around them, watching over them.

Faithfully staying where his master takes him and being consistent to care for his "charges" are Laska's trademarks as a shepherd dog.

They are Sam's hallmarks too as he shepherds his Master's flock. But Sam might face extra temptations to wander because of the special challenges he has. His young church doesn't fit the normal mold. In most cases, before a church is started the main person planting the church builds a core team. He or she gathers anywhere from 10 to 30 people to fill main positions, and everyone moves to the new ministry site together.

Not so at Sam's church. Their core team is still forming. That leaves them with fewer resources in place. For example, they have a worship leader, but no musicians. When they praise God, their only instruments are their voices. But Sam feels that God has given them what they need to do what He has called them to right now.

Sam points out that Laska doesn't pick his job sites. Sam chooses them. Laska works where his master takes him. Sam believes the same is true for him. He believes he is at his church because his Master brought him here. Sam knows he must trust God to provide what he needs, which might not be the same as what Sam thinks he needs.

Sam loves the story of Jesus feeding 5000 people on a mountain because it illustrates that principle (John 6). Jesus and His disciples were at the "job site." A huge crowd gathered to hear Him, and He knew they were hungry. He asked His disciples where they could buy bread to feed the people. They balked at what seemed to them an utterly impossible task. From their perspective even eight months' wages wouldn't buy enough food to fill all those tummies. Okay, so there was a boy with five loaves and two fishes. But that was like one grain of sand on a beach when it came to meeting a huge need like feeding thousands, right?

Wrong! Jesus took this "scarcity," blessed it, and told the disciples to pass out dinner. That measly meal multiplied until all the people, including the disciples, had all the food they needed. As if that weren't enough, there were 12 brimming baskets left over! Jesus showed His disciples that if they were faithful to stay on His job site, He would supply what they needed to fulfill His purposes.

Some people may be lured off God's job site by confusing ministry with career. We may be tempted to wander off when a larger, more prestigious, better paying opportunity beckons... even though God is calling us to stay where we are. And even if we remain on the job, our hearts may wander. God doesn't want that either. He wants us to stay on His job site, giving 100 percent until He takes us to a new one. He calls us to be faithful and to leave the results to Him.

Sam notes that Jesus is the ultimate example of a shepherd who stayed on God's job site. For three and a half years He closely mentored an oddball group of people. They weren't always quick to learn the lessons He sought to teach. And in the end, one betrayed Him while others ran away in His greatest hour of need. But Jesus stayed faithful to His Father's calling, and after He was raised from the dead, His disciples were transformed by His Spirit and went on to turn the world upside down for their Master.

To earthly eyes, Jesus' job site might not have seemed very promising. But God, in His wisdom, knew the blessings and fruit it would yield. Sam trusts that wisdom. He knows his job is to keep showing up and encouraging his small flock. He knows his Master will move him if and when the time is right. Until then, he's determined to stay faithful to the sheep the Lord has entrusted to him. Sam will remain on God's job site for their good and God's glory.

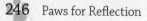

Keep watch over yourselves and all the flock of which the Holy Spirit has made you overseers (Acts 20:28).

Consider This

Are you working on God's job site? What are your greatest challenges there? Are you wholly committed? If your heart has wandered, why is that? How can you adjust your perspective to help you be even more faithful to what God has called you to right now?

Boning Up IV

Special Jobs Dogs Do

1. What are "assistance dogs"? How many ways can you think of that dogs help people with special needs?

2. What job did some dogs once do that was a bit "fishy"?

3. What job do some dogs do that is related to gourmet cooking?

4. What are some ways dogs are used by law enforcement and military personnel?

5. How did some dogs help in space exploration?

Boning Up Answers

Boning Up I: Doggie Body Language

1. In a dog's social order, being in a higher position relative to the dog indicates dominance. Sitting on the floor at a dog's eye level may make fearful dogs feel safer.

2. An intriguing study suggests dogs wag their tails more on the right side of their bodies when they feel positive about a person or animal and more on the left side when they feel negative. According to the researchers quoted in the article we read, it has something to do with brain asymmetry. It can be hard to spot with the naked eye. Why not observe your dog and check it out?

3. Dogs that aren't acquainted with you might interpret a smile as "baring your teeth," an aggressive stance. It could trigger a fight or defensive behavior in dogs.

4. Small children may grab at a dog's muzzle or the nape of its neck. These are areas a mother dog uses to chastise or discipline her pups or assert her leadership. As dogs mature, they often go for these areas when they fight. If a child does this, a dog may feel challenged and/or threatened, which may lead to trouble.

5. Dogs who "just wanna have fun" and play may "bow" by lowering their front ends and keeping their wiggling rumps in the air. They may also bounce, jump, dash back and forth, and run in circles.

Boning Up II: Obedience Training

1. Renaming a dog you've just adopted can help give the dog a fresh start. If the animal has been in an abusive situation, it may associate its old name with negative feedback and actions. Giving it a new name allows the dog to develop positive associations with being called and asked to obey commands.

2. Praising a dog immediately when it does something right, such as obeying

a command, creates a positive association with the desired behavior. When potty-training a puppy, it helps to praise the pup when it does its "business" where you want it to.

3. If you give a dog a command and it doesn't respond immediately, repeating the command one or more additional times may tell the dog it doesn't have to obey the first time. It's better to remain silent after the command, giving the dog more time to respond.

4. If your dog knows the "come" command and it's headed toward danger, you can call it back. "Boundary training" can also keep your dog from harm. If your dog has been trained to "wait" at the threshold of doorways and at street curbs so it doesn't go outside or off the sidewalk without a verbal signal from you, you can better control its behavior and keep the pup from serious trouble.

5. If your puppy gets attention—even negative attention—from jumping up on you, that may reinforce the practice. When it jumps up, look away or walk away. Getting down on the puppy's level when you first teach it to "come" can also forestall "jumping up" behavior. So can teaching your dog to "sit" when it greets you.

Boning Up III: Dogs and Health

1. In the U.S., obesity is the top nutritional problem for dogs. It increases its risk of skeletal, respiratory, and heart problems. If your dog is overweight, talk to your vet about the best plan to correct the situation.

2. If your dog has bad breath, it might need its teeth cleaned. Keeping your dog's teeth and gums in good health is also important because infections in the mouth can lead to infections elsewhere. It can also be painful for the dog.

3. Most people know that chocolate can be toxic to dogs. But so can grapes, raisins, macadamia nuts, onions, and garlic. If you live in an area where mushrooms grow wild, your dog may be at risk of eating poisonous ones. The low-calorie, low-glycemic sweetener xylitol is also poisonous to dogs and can be lethal in tiny amounts. Make sure any food that contains it is kept away

from pups. See your vet for more information on these and other poison hazards.

4. On a warm day the temperature in a parked car can soar much higher than the outdoor temperature, even if the vehicle is in the shade. In just minutes pets can suffocate or succumb to heat stroke.

5. The culprit for most dog allergy sufferers is a protein found in the animals' dander, saliva, and urine. There is no truly nonallergenic (allergy free) dog. Some breeds are allegedly less likely to cause allergies, but this is disputed. There is no hard scientific evidence to that effect. Individual allergy sufferers whose problems are mild may find a particular dog they can tolerate. There are also ways to minimize allergens in homes where dogs live. Consult your physician and follow his or her recommendations.

Boning Up IV: Special Jobs Dogs Do

1. There are many types of "assistance dogs" that aid people with special needs. Guide dogs are partnered with the blind or partially blind to enhance mobility. Hearing dogs alert deaf or hard-of-hearing individuals to sounds around them, such as a doorbell or ringing phone. Service dogs do various tasks for people with physical disabilities, such as picking up objects, opening doors, and turning on lights. Dogs have also been trained to help people with epilepsy and autism.

2. Ancestors of the Labrador retriever once helped Newfoundland fishermen by retrieving fishing nets and lines. Characteristics such as webbed toes and a double-layered coat (the top part repels water) made them well-suited to going into the water.

3. In Europe dogs and pigs are used to sniff out rare edible fungi called "truffles," which are highly prized and used in gourmet cooking. The animals dig up the underground truffles. However, pigs are more apt to eat the truffles they find than dogs are.

4. Dogs perform many valuable jobs for law enforcement and the military. They sniff for bombs, drugs, and even "forbidden fruit" or food items someone

may be bringing into the country illegally. Dogs have also been trained to aid in search-and-rescue operations and to track missing persons and escaped prisoners. One dog has even helped its archaeologist master on digs by sniffing out the bones of people who've been dead for centuries.

5. In the early days of space exploration, the USSR sent dogs up to see if traveling into space was feasible for humans. Dogs went on suborbital and orbital flights. Some survived their trips, but others didn't. The first earth creature other than microbes to orbit the earth was a dog named Laika, who flew on Sputnik 2 (November 3, 1957). Sadly, she didn't live to "bark the tale."

Dog Tails...er, Tales by Author

Connie Fleishauer

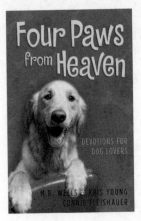

Four Paws from Heaven
Devotions for Dog Lovers

Life is better with a dog! Friend, family member, guardian, comforter—a dog can add so much to our lives. These furry, four-footed creatures truly are wonderful gifts from a loving Creator to bring joy, laughter, and warmth to our hearts and homes. Sometimes they do seem "heaven sent."

These fun and furry devotions will make you smile and perhaps grow a little misty-eyed as you enjoy true stories of how God watches over and provides for us even as we care for our canine companions. Experience warm moments of connection with Him as you consider...

- how a little obedience can keep you from danger
- why trusting your Master is always a good thing to do
- how just being with God is the best possible place to be

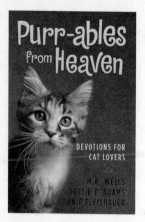

Purr-ables from Heaven
Devotions for Cat Lovers

Life is purr-fect with a cat! For those with the right cat-itude, there is nothing like a nice kitty to make life great. When Muffin, Pumpkin, and Milkshake p-u-r-r-r-r out their love for you, your heart just melts. Then they're off chasing a butterfly, stalking a squirrel, or sleeping in a patch of warm sunlight. They may be independent at times, but when they want to, they can wrap you around their little paws. Cat people love cats not because they are purr-fect, but in spite of their flaws.

Perhaps humans are more like cats than they realize when it comes to relating to a loving Master. These entertaining and enlightening devotions will delight you as you discover how God daily...

- draws you to Himself
- provides for your every need
- loves you purr-fectly in spite of your flaws